TRANSFORMATIONAL SANCTUARIES IN THE MIDDLE LEVEL ELA CLASSROOM

Drawing from an arts-based research and humanizing methodologies, Dywanna Smith documents transformative and liberatory spaces in ELA middle level classrooms, where students address and counteract discrimination, colorism, sizism, and body shaming. Grounded in an original qualitative study of adolescent Black girls, this book examines how such "truth spaces" serve as a medium for adolescents to self-examine their intersectional identities and give voice to their resilience in the face of marginalization.

Incorporating original narratives, including the author's self-actualizing verse novel and the voices of Black female students, Smith shines a light on new culturally sustaining pedagogies and offers much-needed implications for practice. Smith expertly weaves together poetry, research, and empathy; the result is a pioneering text that urges readers to understand the impact of anti-Black violence and the important role literacy sanctuaries can play in supporting Black girls' resilience and development. The novel in verse at the heart of the volume is not only a provocative and necessary call for transformative change, but also a window into a courageous lived experience. This book is essential reading for pre-service teachers, scholars, and students in literacy education, inclusive education, and teacher education.

Dywanna E. Smith is Assistant Professor of Education at Claflin University, where she serves as Middle Level Education Program Coordinator and Interim Assessment Coordinator.

NCTE-Routledge Research Series
Series Editors: Valerie Kinloch and Susi Long

Brooks
Transforming Literacy Education for Long-Term English Learners: Recognizing Brilliance in the Undervalued

Baker-Bell
Linguistic Justice: Black Language, Literacy, Identity, and Pedagogy

Nash, Polson, Glover
Toward Culturally Sustaining Teaching: Early Childhood Educators Honor Children with Practices for Equity and Change

Bryan
Toward a BlackBoyCrit Pedagogy: Black Boys, Male Teachers, and Early Childhood Classroom Practices

Johnson
Critical Race English Education: New Visions, New Possibilities

Smith
Transformational Sanctuaries in the Middle Level ELA Classroom: Creating Truth Spaces for Black Girls

---

The NCTE-Routledge Research Series, copublished by the National Council of Teachers of English and Routledge, focuses on literacy studies in P-12 classroom and related contexts. Volumes in this series are invited publications or publications submitted in response to a call for manuscripts. They are primarily authored or co-authored works which are theoretically significant and broadly relevant to the P-12 literacy community. The series may also include occasional landmark compendiums of research.

The scope of the series includes qualitative and quantitative methodologies; a range of perspectives and approaches (e.g., sociocultural, cognitive, feminist, linguistic, pedagogical, critical, historical, anthropological); and research on diverse populations, contexts (e.g., classrooms, school systems, families, communities), and forms of literacy (e.g., print, electronic, popular media).

TRANSFORMATIONAL SANCTUARIES IN THE MIDDLE LEVEL ELA CLASSROOM

Creating Truth Spaces for Black Girls

Dywanna E. Smith

NEW YORK AND LONDON

Cover image: Painting by Dr. Grace Player

First published 2022
by Routledge
605 Third Avenue, New York, NY 10158

and by Routledge
4 Park Square, Milton Park, Abingdon, Oxon, OX14 4RN

Routledge is an imprint of the Taylor & Francis Group, an informa business

© 2022 Taylor & Francis

The right of Dywanna E. Smith to be identified as author of this work has been asserted in accordance with sections 77 and 78 of the Copyright, Designs and Patents Act 1988.

All rights reserved. No part of this book may be reprinted or reproduced or utilised in any form or by any electronic, mechanical, or other means, now known or hereafter invented, including photocopying and recording, or in any information storage or retrieval system, without permission in writing from the publishers.

Trademark notice: Product or corporate names may be trademarks or registered trademarks, and are used only for identification and explanation without intent to infringe.

Library of Congress Cataloging-in-Publication Data
A catalog record for this title has been requested

ISBN: 978-0-367-35545-6 (hbk)
ISBN: 978-0-367-35544-9 (pbk)
ISBN: 978-0-429-34016-1 (ebk)

DOI: 10.4324/9780429340161

Typeset in Bembo
by SPi Technologies India Pvt Ltd (Straive)

CONTENTS

List of Illustrations   *vi*
Preface: Wanted: Educator Activists Seeking Transformation   *vii*
Acknowledgments   *xi*
Series Editors' Foreword   *xiii*
Author Biography   *xvii*

1. Demanding Truth Spaces: Tell Me How I Stay Positive When They Never See the Good in Me   1

2. Gems of Truth: Research Partners as Love Advocates   12

3. Fake Love: The Truth Behind the Caring Myth   26

4. Stepping Behind the Veil: A Methodology for Crafting a Loving Sanctuary   51

5. Poetic Justice: Truth Revealed in Verse   68

6. You Can't Heal What You Don't Reveal: Ethnopoetics as Truth, Resilience, and Resistance   106

7. "Quiet as It's Kept": Teachers as Truth Warriors Moving Forward with Urgency   146

Appendix   *159*
Index   *167*

LIST OF ILLUSTRATIONS

Figures
3.1	Theoretical Framework	35
4.1	Media Center Conference Room	54
4.2	Journaling Supplies	57
4.3	Partners with Research Supplies	58
6.1	Text Annotation Revision Strategy	110
6.2	Meme Activity	119
6.3	Skin Tone Scale	124
6.4	Black Literary Heritage	141
7.1	Vision Board: Words of Wisdom from My Village	147

Tables
3.1	Reflections on Truth and Love	43
4.1	Text Selection	55
4.2	Descriptive Codes Used for Data Analysis	61
6.1	Characterization Chart	112
6.2	Word Association Responses	115
6.3	Visual Image Responses	116
6.4	Meme Analysis	120
6.5	Body Satisfaction/Dissatisfaction Responses	134
6.6	Power Playlist	139

PREFACE: WANTED: EDUCATOR ACTIVISTS SEEKING TRANSFORMATION

I get it.
I'm young.
You take one look at me
and somehow ascertain
that I don't know much about this world.
I could declare flawed vision and faulty logic,
but I have a question I'm dying to ask.
I know I am supposed
to sit quietly and just
copy down notes
but I can't keep this inside.
So, against this culture
of silence and complacency,
I am going to dare to raise my hand
because I just want to know one thing.
I humbly ask you:
What is so difficult
about seeing me in my totality?
I know I am asking
that you look beyond
test scores;
because how dare you
reduce the brilliance
of my life to the
summation of a performance

on a singular occasion.
I.
Am.
More.
Than.
A.
Mere
Number.

I stand before you brazenly beautiful
drenched in melanin;
a sun-kissed nectar from God.
My skin is portraiture;
a tapestry of art.
I am the essence of creativity.
Unbound Energy.
My spirit is comprised of
movement and song.
Do you know how hard it is
to sit still when my heartbeat
is a drum and my spirit craves
movement?
Chile please!
Give me some space because I need to dance!
Drop!
Bop!
Juju on that beat!
You ain't know I was multilingual did ya?
Dance is just one of the many languages
I speak!

I am expressive!
I am both poet and storyteller.
My heritage can be traced
through the words that I let
slip from tongue.
I inhale my history.
It enriches my form
and I exhale radical hope and possibility.
You see a vessel waiting to be filled
but I am intellect and wisdom.
Science and philosophy
were conceived in my womb.

> You cannot teach
> what you cannot see.
> I am demanding
> you see me.
> Acknowledge me.
> Respect me.
> Love me as I love myself.
>
> I deserve more than a teacher.
> I want an educator activist
> a.k.a. the transformative warrior.
> This work **is not** for everyone.
> It really is simple.
> Those who will not demand
> equity and excellence
> when educating African American students
> need
> not
> apply.

This Book

I offer this book as a call to action to educators whose job is to advocate, listen, instruct, support, nurture, protect and love young Black women in classrooms in a society filled with the reification of whiteness, thinness, and dominance by men. I do so using poetry as well as narrative, both are languages of my heart and mind. Both forms allow me to express realities in ways that I hope will have an impact on readers' hearts and minds, leading you to consider what those realities mean for your own classroom and educational institution.

This work demands a willing and compassionate heart. Each chapter was written to push forward critical introspective into your beliefs, ideals, and pedagogical practices by sharing my own experiences, the work and words of scholars who illuminate issues around Black assault and Black love, and my collaboration with five young Black women as we engaged together in an afterschool critical literacy study group. In vulnerable transparency, Chapter 1 uses my personal history to contextualize how I came to this research and why it is so desperately needed. Chapter 2 introduces the five young women who are the heart of this book and describes the naming of our literature study group which became a truth space for all of us. It also sets the scene for the rest of the book by offering a research-based discussion of why these stories matter for adolescent Black women and the teachers, administrators, and teacher educators who impact their lives. Chapter 3 contextualizes the plight of Black girls within the notions of fake and real love by connecting realities during the COVID-19 pandemic with current and historical assault on Blackness followed by the Black scholar wisdom that guides me. Chapter 4 delves into the heart of the process of creating and sustaining a truth space. Chapter 5 reveals the findings from our truth space in ethnopoetic form, a chapter that I invite you to reread multiple times as it needs to be internalized slowly; and the young women's lives deserve repeated attention. Chapter 6 explains the art of creating the poems while taking readers deeper into our teaching and learning experiences. Usually, when reading in a linear fashion, you would move to Chapter 6. I ask though, that you revisit Chapter 5 to delve deeper into the metacognitive processes which provoked poetic findings. The truths within these chapters don't always unfold in a linear fashion, which is fine as research doesn't occur in a linear fashion but as a cycle. At times, we have to revisit certain moments within the cycle, each visitation nurtures a new interpretation. I ask that you revisit Chapter 5 in hopes that, with a deeper context, new understandings will spring forth. I also make this request because Black female lives are worthy of reimagination, redefining, relistening, revaluation, remembering, and being retroactively allowed to move freely beyond society's margins. Chapter 6 explains how each poem was carefully crafted and how this genre ushered our personal liberation. Finally, Chapter 7 concludes the book with implications for personal and pedagogical change.

As you move into these chapters, it will be important to remember that it is not by chance that many Black girls never see themselves revered and loved in classrooms. It was and is NOT by chance. It was born of strategy throughout history meant to keep whiteness supreme. To deny this truth is to be complicit in another's subjugation. To deny this truth is to place your privilege and security over another's need for justice. I humbly submit that you consider this book as Auntie Maxine Waters would say a "reclaiming of time," memories, stories, truths, and love. Black girlhood is revolutionary and should be perceived and celebrated as such. With these words, I ask that you see this book and the research behind it not as a place to hide, but instead, a place to celebrate and explore the realities of six Black girls, each demanding to be seen, heard, and validated and then to use this work to demand and enact change.

ACKNOWLEDGMENTS

I began this journey with many uncertainties. I end it strong, proud, and filled with love because my village has centered and grounded me. Thank you to my village for carrying me through the difficult times, celebrating my successes, and loving me regardless. I could not have done this without you. This work stands testimony to the power of faith. Some of those people are (**in no particular order**):

Eugene and Ellen Marie Smith
Donna Smith
Darrin & Rhea Smith
Drs. Dwight Smith & Leslie Rivera
Arlyn, Aaliyah, & Aubrey Alfred
Cameron Smith
Geraldine Jones (aka The Fourth Smith Traveler)
Shanise Brown
The Smith/Jones Family Collective
My Heavenly Ancestors (Roosevelt, Venia, Ernest, Carrie, Eugene, Isabelle, David, Eddie, Holland, George, Virginia, Mattie, Dusty, Amos, May, Dot, and Wayne)
Dr. Susi Long
Dr. Valerie Kinloch
Dr. Gloria Boutte
Dr. Tasha Laman
Dr. Toni Williams
Dr. Grace Player
Dr. George Johnson
Dr. Ronnie Hopkins
Dr. Lamar Johnson
Dr. Nathaniel Bryan

Dr. Jennifer Wilson
Dr. Anthony Broughton
Dr. Anthony A. Pittman
Mr. Demeturia Kelly
The Claflin University Family & Dr. Dwaun J. Warmack
Claflin University School of Education
Claflin University Middle Level Majors
Dr. Venus Evans-Winters
Dr. Sakeena Everett
Dr. Gwenda Greene
Dr. Damara Hightower-Mitchell
Antoinette, Jeff, and Xander (My Love) Mursier
Janice Baines
Saudah Collins
Canisha Fletcher
Dr. Tori Simmons
Karis Mazyck
James D. Barr
Spencer "Chad" Jasper
Kelvin Griffin Jr.
Jarvais Jackson
Ricardo Robinson
Robert Leon Dennis
CNV Cohort
Linda and Travis Chatman
Dec. Willie T. and Patricia Brown
Dec. Napoleon and Luellen Brown
Mt. Olive Baptist Church Family
Ms. Lizzie Barr and Ms. Lula Tisdale
The Black Girls' Literacies Collective
FOCs
My sisters of Alpha Eta and the Delta Kappa Gamma International Society and the many others who helped along the way
Special Thanks to my Blue Diamond Girls for proudly loving and embracing your Blackness. I have grown more as a scholar and love advocate by listening to your stories:

I've cried alongside each of you.
Been both broken and reborn.
Baptized by the power of Black love and resilience,
I listened attentively and was
drenched in wisdom.
Your stories are my roots.

SERIES EDITORS' FOREWORD

> I am both poet and storyteller.
> My heritage can be traced
> through the words that I let
> slip from tongue.
> I inhale my history.
> It enriches my form
> and I exhale radical hope and possibility.
> You see a vessel waiting to be filled
> but I am intellect and wisdom.

Dywanna Smith crafted the words in the above poem that opens this book, words that reflect the courage, purpose, heart, rigor, and insight with which she constructed this incredible volume. Smith is indeed a powerful poet and a storyteller who captures the heart of pedagogy, teaching, research, and activism as she urges us to transform systems that try to destroy the lives, hearts, and spirits of Black girls. We could not agree more wholeheartedly with the words of one of the book's reviewers who eloquently described the experience of reading this book:

> It was an absolute joy. A spirit-filling, mind-engaging, futures-creating joy. One part memoir, one part poetry anthology, one part research study and one part handbook for those who want to pour into the lives, hearts and minds of Black girls in humanizing ways. Dr. Smith's selfless sharing of her own life experiences gives an in-depth exposure to one Black girl that can be informative for the many. The intersectional nexus of race, gender and body size explored with this level of intricacy and through the lens of youths is a needed and exciting contribution to the field. Dr. Smith has

channeled the spirit of the fingers of the ancestors and used them to weave together the many literacy expressions contained in this book into a tapestry of Black girl beauty and joy, and I am SO here for it!

It is not an overstatement to say that this volume is outstanding, given its expert melding of verse, narrative, experience, research, literature, wisdom, and activism. A must-read for teachers, teacher educators, administrators, and educational researchers, it is crafted with brilliance, depth, and radical love, and it represents the highest levels of rigor in pedagogy, educational research, and representation (for researchers, Smith includes an Appendix that shares a detailed methodological process).

Within these pages, Smith draws us into the worlds of five Black middle school girls as they collectively created "truth spaces"—sanctuaries for examining issues of body image, race, gender, and literacy in an afterschool program. In the process, Smith and the Blue Diamonds—the self-named group, came to see their critical literacy sanctuary as space "for resilience, rejuvenation, and revitalizing education." Situated within an afterschool program, Smith urges us to see such spaces as vital to daily classroom life in order to counter the "precarious position [of Black girls] in America: their stories silenced, their bodies objectified, brutalized, and murdered."

Readers will enter this volume with tremendous anticipation as Smith invites us into her own life experiences and then into the worlds of the Blue Diamonds. We gain insights into teaching and learning as we watch the Blue Diamonds grow as readers, writers, thinkers, conceptualizers, creators, and activists. In ways that no other pedagogical or research text has done before, Smith sculpts life, research, and pedagogy into both poetry and narrative to vividly communicate experience, wisdom, practice, history, and theory. In a "critical act of resistance," Smith asks readers to fully reject colonized structures for presenting research and practice; in this asking, she creates a text that envelops readers within the writing, graphic representation, verbalization, and performances of the Blue Diamonds. Poetry is a primary lens Smith uses to "analyze and interpret the world... as an offering to teachers who have the power to make a difference in the lives of students most oppressed." As a result, we come away with deeper understandings of ourselves, our perceptions, and the urgent need for productive change in the teaching of Black girls.

After meeting Smith and the Blue Diamonds in the opening chapters, she takes us into Chapter 3 to offer a deep and searing exploration of love: *Fake Love* that merely perpetuates white supremacy and anti-Black violence in schools and society; and the *Thick Love, Radical Love* that is needed in every classroom. Questions are posed that inspire us to examine our personal and professional choices as they do or do not reflect Fake as well as Thick and Radical Love. The inspiration of "literary giants" are drawn into the narrative, compelling us to release past assumptions about acts of love and to understand what it means to "walk in love in times when [we are] least hopeful about the world's destruction of Blackness." Chapter 4 offers rich descriptions of critical literacy engagements, anchored in Thick Radical Love, that took place in the Blue Diamonds' afterschool Truth Spaces. It included a curriculum involving photos, discussion questions, texts, the girls' creation of counternarratives, journaling, and analytical processes.

Then, there is the exquisite Chapter 5, a Novel in Verse. This chapter emerges as a series of poems that are at the same time explosive, gentle, intuitive, courageous, informative, and provocative. This chapter powerfully speaks to every classroom teacher, teacher educator, and educational researcher. Crafted from the experiences of the Blue Diamonds, Smith's notes as a teacher and researcher, and the language of theory and pedagogy, the poems are truths that every educator should hear and feel. This is a chapter that should be read again and again as, each time, readers absorb more and more from its power, beauty, and message. In the chapter that follows, Smith unpacks each poem, describing the process of reflection and analysis that resulted in the creation of the poems, taking us even further into her work with the Blue Diamonds and the urgent need for transformation in the education of Black girls. The book closes with strong and necessary implications for educators, asking us to "stare deeply into the depths of [our] souls" as we engage in self-examination as well as the development of classrooms as sanctuaries for Black girls.

We are beyond proud that *Transformational Sanctuaries in the Middle Level ELA Classroom: Creating Truth Spaces for Black Girls* joins the books in our NCTE-Routledge Research Series. It enriches our commitment to books that take a critical look at classroom practice and research, and that speak to the ways in which each must attend to the lives of People of Color within and beyond P-12 classrooms. Smith's text joins books carefully selected for authors' commitments to the educators' role in moving us toward a more equitable society in a series that includes foci on equity, justice, and antiracist education; critical qualitative, quantitative, and mixed methodologies; a range of cutting-edge approaches (e.g., sociocultural, cognitive, feminist, linguistic, pedagogical, critical, historical, anthropological); and research on the literacies of minoritized peoples as well as on diverse contexts (e.g., classrooms, school systems, families, communities) and forms of literacy (e.g., print, electronic, popular media).

We hope that, through Smith's work, you are moved to action in your own educational setting as you "celebrate and explore the realities of... Black girls, each demanding to be seen, heard, and validated and then [using] this work to demand and enact change." Dive deeply into the poetry that will guide you from beginning to end. Engage in the heart work necessary to see the depth of experiential, theoretical, methodological, analytical, and academic orientation that makes this volume so important in the work to recreate schools as places of truth and love, and as you consider your role as an educator activist. Keep the voices of the Blue Diamonds close to your heart as, through Smith's poetry, they call for action from educators everywhere:

I am demanding
you see me.
Acknowledge me.
Respect me.
Love me as I love myself.

I deserve more than a teacher.
I want an educator activist
a.k.a. the transformative warrior.

Valerie Kinloch
Renée and Richard Goldman Dean and Professor of Education
University of Pittsburgh
USA

and

Susi Long
Professor, Instruction and Teacher Education
University of South Carolina, Columbia
USA

AUTHOR BIOGRAPHY

Dr. Dywanna E. Smith is an Assistant Professor of Education at Claflin University, where she serves as Middle Level Education Program Coordinator and Interim Assessment Coordinator. She received her doctorate in language and literacy from the University of South Carolina. Her dissertation interpreted how eighth-grade African American girls perceived obesity in their daily lives and analyzed what happened when opportunities were given to create counternarratives about race, gender, and size. Informed by Critical Race Theory and Black Feminist Theory, the study centered the body as a textual artifact, broadened notions of what counts as text which can be critically read, and provided models for nurturing youth in tackling school and community issues.

As a scholar-educator, Dr. Smith's research focuses on two related interests: 1) examining the intersections of race, literacies, and education and 2) equipping teachers with equity pedagogies to successfully teach linguistically and culturally diverse students. She has presented nationally and internationally on these subjects.

Dr. Smith's work is grounded in ethnopoetics. She utilizes poetry to speak to the realities of Black girls and women and to resist and respond to racism, sexism, sizism, and misogynoir. Her co-edited book project, *African Diaspora Literacy: The Heart of Transformation in K–12 Schools and Teacher Education,* alongside Drs. Lamar Johnson, Gloria Boutte, and Gwenda Greene, is a 2019 American Educational Studies Association (AESA) Critics Choice Book Award Winner.

Dr. Smith is a Fulbright Scholar Project Participant and a graduating member of the National Council of English's prestigious Cultivating New Voices among Scholars of Color (CNV) program. She is also a member of the Justice as Praxis in Education Collective (JPEC).

1
DEMANDING TRUTH SPACES

Tell Me How I Stay Positive When They Never See the Good in Me

odo nyera

Your words communed with my spirit,
eulogized doubt and insecurities
and prophesied my emotional resurrection.
I became the prodigal daughter
and returned home to my heart.
There I nested in love.
-emergence

Dywanna Smith, August 2017

I stood naked staring at my reflection in my parent's bathroom mirror. The face peering at me was both a friend as well as a stranger. While I gazed, tears streamed down her immense Black cheeks. Her mouth twisted in pain. Though she did not speak, I knew her story – bearing the torment of classmates, friends, yelling "Fatso," calling her ugly, reminding her she could be beautiful, "if only she lost weight." Her corpulent form was foreign and alien. The mounds of fat repulsed her. If she could, she would be willing to take a knife and carve the vile deformities from her flesh. They preyed on her consuming her inch by inch – an omniscient presence reminding her that she was Not normal. She was Not beautiful. She was NOT allowed. What is the point of living if society denies you entrance?

Her gaze drops to the countertop, and she stares at the pain medication, knowing the small, round white capsules can be both savior and escape. Unflinchingly, she pours the pills into her hand. As she slowly reaches to taste salvation, her father's footsteps can be heard in the hallway coming closer. Soon, his strong Black fists are pounding on the door, and he yells in a deep baritone, "Dee! Dee! You should be ready by now! Hurry up!" She stops. There is a moment of awareness – a moment of recognition that the man who cared for her and loved her would find her lifeless body. Once again, she stares at the capsules and though life was too much to live for herself, she realized she would try to do it for him. She pours the pills back into the bottle. As they hit the brown plastic, their soft taps seem to call to her, tempting her back into their power. They whisper to her, "Only in death and darkness will you find acceptance." She closes the pill bottle to silence their temptation and looks in the mirror at her deep caramel skin, her repulsive fat curves, and cries; her anguish eclipsing her resolve.

Learning to Hate Myself: Ingesting Dominant Ideology

As a child growing up in Kingstree, SC, I remembered being surrounded by family and friends – all faces that looked like mine and reflected my beauty. I can remember walking hand in hand with my grandmother and loving the variations in hues of skin – my tawny brown against her dark black leather – aged, cracked, yet perfectly soft. I wrapped myself in bear hugs from my uncles whose skin resembled the midnight sky. My family taught me how to love my body. I never once heard the word fat; instead, my family, in Black English that constituted the sounds of love and home and community always said, "Ain't she fine." Their words embraced my body and I knew that I was beautiful.

At first, I thought these carefully timed events were fortuitous; but age brings wisdom and hindsight often refines our vision until that which was once indistinct becomes focused and rich. The fond memories my family so carefully wove were not chance; they were by strategic creation. It was not by chance that every face I saw in magazines in my household looked like mine. My mother dusted the coffee table and tucked the *Good Housekeeping* behind the couch so my brothers, sister, and I could stare at the faces on *Ebony* and *Jet Magazines*. Family pictures decorated our halls to show that beauty was not static; it was fluidic and came in a variety of hues and forms. It was not by chance I never had a white doll baby as a child. I loved peering into the dark brown eyes of my Cabbage Patch Doll, Ezmeralda, because she looked like me. It was not by chance we studied Black scientists, authors, poets so that we could know despite everything; some people sacrificed their lives, so we could move our people further. It was not by chance, it was strategy; because my parents fully realized when I left my home's refuge, I would be besieged by a powerful discourse of hate. So, they taught me early, how to love my Blackness.

Their strategy worked well as I learned what Black was by learning from close family. It was only until I started middle school that the strategy needed to be reworked. Until my sixth-grade year, many of my teachers were Black plus-sized women – the only exception being my second-grade teacher as she was a tall thin white woman. As I was growing up, it was not a thought on which I tarried long. It was simply a portion of my existence, my Kingstree if you will. I cannot remember being teased about my size in primary school. In fact, my teachers' mere presence dared any student to try taunts or insults. They would move their large bodies between desks and chairs with the poise and confidence of African dancers. With hands placed upon hips, students were reminded to remember their place. Their smiles lay firmly placed between dimpled cheeks. They embodied beauty. How could I not be beautiful when surrounded by such women?

During sixth grade, everything changed. I had the first of several white teachers and somehow things shifted. Teachers whose very presence modeled the message that beauty comes in every size disappeared. I was surrounded by thinness and those who were not thin discussed their plans for obtaining the ideal. I would overhear conversations about dieting and the need to get back into some former size. I cannot pinpoint when it began, but I do remember my classmates teasing me. The boys were especially cruel. They would call me "fatty" and pull at my dresses. One classmate, Xavier (pseudonym), was especially mean-spirited. He would stand behind me and mimic my walk extending his arms wide and inhaling air until his cheeks puffed. Teasing my fat was not just a hobby; to him, it was a full-time occupation.

The memories are still vivid in my mind. Xavier would always start his comedic routine by screaming, "Boom! Boom!" I tried to imagine the sound of thunder shattering the sky. I tried to pretend I was such a powerful and dynamic force, but my musings were always interrupted by snickers and howling laughter. "Boom! Boom!" One would think at some time the joke would get old, but apparently like the classic black dress or vintage cars, some jokes were timeless. That Monday, as with any other day, my attempts to walk to class were a cause for hilarity. Perhaps, it was because my body jiggled while others had a smooth gait. I never fully understood. I just wanted to be in the safety of the classroom, huddled at a desk, longing to be invisible. But Xavier's deafening screams would only increase. "Boom! Boom! E-A-R-T-H-Q-U-A-K-E!" By then, others joined in on the joke. They would grab onto their book bags and pretend to lose their equilibrium.

At times, I wished I were an earthquake. I wished I could split the earth and fall between its crevices, but I did not possess that power. I only possessed the power to continue walking: to put one foot in front of the other, to finally cross the threshold of safety. In such awful times, tears were not an option, as they only mark you as prey. Instead, I walked bravely over to my desk removing books, preparing for class, pretending not to care. I was a master pretender. Like many before me, I wore "the mask that grins and lies" (Dunbar, 1969). My mask of stoicism was so firmly planted; I often fooled myself. At some point, my emotions flooded their fragile banks, the mask dropped, and reality crept into being. I could no longer pretend I was not injured or scarred; because inwardly I recognized, I was damaged goods. I was left only wondering if I would ever heal.

I knew my teacher heard his teasing. Once I even witnessed her turn her head to laugh. She did precious little to protect me. When I approached her about it privately, she pointedly told me, "I needed to develop thicker skin because life was tough." My world folded. My supposed advocate betrayed me. I dropped my head and started walking out of the classroom, determined for her not to see my tears. Although I resolved to be strong, she noticed my slumped shoulders and called me back over to her. She leaned down gently rubbed my face and said, "Sweetie, if you don't like them teasing you, you can do something. You can lose weight." Somehow, in the span of a few short years, I drifted from being someone beautiful to some "thing" needing to be fixed. That day, everything changed, and my teacher opened my eyes to sizism and hate.

My journey into the actualization I feel today and through which I can write this book was derailed because of events like these and those that followed. In the next two years, I learned to abhor my body and view it as foreign and grotesque. I did not realize it at the time, as I ingested food for nourishment; I also internalized Western beauty standards. I learned that Barbie dolls, with their long glossy blond hair, striking blue eyes and tiny cinched waists, closely resembled perfection and my rotund form was the direct opposite. The language I used to describe myself changed from "fine" to thinking of my chipmunk cheeks, pudgy hands, and elephantine buttocks. The cruel insults thrown at me every day just reinforced that the larger world around me did not believe that I was "fine." At 12, I would duck into closets or hide behind locked doors to grieve. I would scream into towels and wipe tears from my face. I carried this self-loathing internally for years, diving into darkness and depression.

The darkness continued well into junior high. I tried to find solace by joining the school newspaper, thinking the clever wordplay and creativity would shield me. I clung to words as my lifeboat, finding temporary relief. My counselor noticed my low self-esteem and advised my teachers to allow me leadership duties. I became an office courier, assisted with bulletin boards, and helped organize school events. It was here that my lifeboat disappeared. While working in a teacher's classroom, an adolescent boy assaulted me. I was left feeling vulnerable and violated. I have often tried to write or discuss the experience and my words will not come in a prose story-telling fashion. They come in short, stilted phrases. I grasped at each phrase for 25 years and finally, finally, I could weave that horrific event into a poem. It is not prose, but it is my testimony and truth:

> Power?
> Power is only having your words as weapons.
> Power is saying that if I did not do
> EXACTLY
> as you demanded,
> YOU would ruin
> My NAME.
> My name…
> the one thing in this world I was freely given.
>
> Power?
> Power is looking me in the face,

watching my disbelief,
and allowing your
words to create
an atmosphere of fear
which sweetly suffocates.
One …
to which I foolishly succumbed.

Power?
Power is making me doubt myself;
making me question the audacity of my voice.
My actions were paradoxical.
Slow labored and ragged breaths
juxtaposed by
thoughts rushing through my mind;
Most of which were
a torrent of your vulgarities:
"Who would believe you?"
"It's your fault anyway!"
"They will think you lied!"
"Why would anyone want you fatty?"
"You know you Black girls are always so damn fast…"
My head was a tornado of confusion.
Thoughts moving so swiftly,
they crashed into each other
and a headache ensued.
I clutched my head between my hands
trying to shake loose this horrid experience,
no relief comes.

Power?
Is a vice-grip!
Your power takes hold…
Seizing me.
Tearing into me.
You don't even have to speak.
Your eyes compel me to kneel.
It's not who I am
It's not what I want to be doing.
Yet… it's who I am forced to become.
More pain.
More ragged breaths.
More horrific silence.

I cry afterward.
But you'll never know that.
Even if you did,
you would not have cared.
Because you were…
Consumed with power.
Enamored with power.
Infected by power.
My subjugation only
fueled a ravenous appetite.
Afterward, you sat stuffed,
victoriously sated.
While I …
I was instantly debilitated.
Decades have passed,
and I am both
scarred;
yet, mercifully healed.
Decades have passed.
and
I can still feel your power.

I never told anyone. I kept this secret from family and friends. I silently berated myself for being so naïve. My assault was my mistake. His words were knives to my spirit. I internalized his venomous verbiage. I was one of those promiscuous Black girls. I was fat and hideous – yet another experience moving further away from being "so fine." Who would believe me because no one, at least no one in their right mind, would want me? This was indeed my fault and I hated myself for it. The once-happy and dedicated student transformed into a sullen and depressed girl. I wanted to fade away from existence. I withdrew from my friends and family and tried to find comfort in isolation. I wore a well-constructed mask and I played my part so well, I lost myself in the pretend role.

During that time, the one reassuring space in my school life was in the classroom of my eighth-grade English teacher: Mrs. Roberts. Mrs. Roberts was a force to which to be reckoned. She stood five feet six inches tall with dark ebony skin and high heels. She was one of the few Black teachers I encountered that year. When she spoke, she commanded respect. She greeted each student at her door with a smile and took time to ask about our siblings, many of whom she had taught. Her class became my sanctuary.

It was there that I fell hopelessly in love with English/language arts. We did not read a text; we experienced it through role-play, music, and art. I became an educator because I wanted to be Mrs. Roberts. This was the one time of the day where I allowed myself to smile – at least until the assault. Afterward, I did not often speak in class. I did not raise my hand to answer questions or to take part in role-playing. I complied and completed every assignment. My body was present, but my mind was not and although I was like this in all my classes, it was Mrs. Roberts who reached out to me. I am alive because she gave me poetry as a saving grace.

One day after class, Mrs. Roberts asked me to stay back. Ashamed, I hung my head. I was not used to being chastised by a teacher. I remember watching her walk over to the door and softly close it. She then walked slowly to my desk where I tried to make the desktop my horizon, gazing squarely at it. She reached out, gently took my chin in her hands, and lifted my head until I looked her squarely in the eyes. With her other hand, she cupped my cheek and said,

> My darling, I am going to lose you and I do not want that to happen. I don't know what happened to you, but I know you are in a lot of pain and if you do not find some way to release it, I will be attending your funeral and I love you too much to see that happen.

I was astounded. How did she know my secret? How did she know that the tiny capsules were still calling my name and trying to tempt me to death? She read the truth in my eyes and released my face. Once again, I watched her motions as she traveled to her desk and opened its drawer. From its depths, she pulled a spiral notebook with a purple cover: My first truth space. Her heels clicked on the floor as she walked back over to me. She placed the notebook in my hands, and said one word, "Write." With tears streaming down my face, I softly replied, "I don't have the words. I don't know what to say."

I thought this revelation would end the conversation and I turned my body to try to leave my desk and the notebook. Mrs. Roberts did not allow me to move, she placed her body in front of the desk as a deterrent. Once again, she picked up the notebook forced it into my clenched hands. Once again, she said,

> Write. Repeat that phrase over and over into this notebook until something comes. My child, you are in pain. There is something inside of you that wants to be released and if you are not going to speak that pain, then you must write it.

I realized that my escape would only come if I took ownership of the notebook. I did not want the burden of writing, but I kept the notebook in my hands. Only then did Mrs. Roberts move, and I quickly fled from the classroom.

Despite my angst, I went home and tried to write, but the words would not come. Yet, I remembered Mrs. Roberts' advice and I wrote, "I don't have the words. I don't know what to say" over and over in my notebook. My handwriting shifted from a practiced scrawl to a feverish frenzy because as I filled each line in the notebook my rage swelled and before my body realized it, my mind began to release the rage. I could not form complete sentences, but the words grouped together formed phrases. It was incomplete. It was imperfect; yet, I put pen to paper.

The next day, I did not speak to Mrs. Roberts. I arrived for class early and placed the notebook on her desk. While we completed an assignment, I noticed she picked up my notebook and began to read. I felt vulnerable as her eyes darted across the lines. My thoughts settled on the imperfections of the writing. There was no topic sentence and I had not used vivid words, nor did I utilize transitions. As an essay, it was disastrous. When she finished reading, Mrs. Roberts placed the notebook on the desk. Her face was stoic but I knew, I just knew, I had failed my task.

She didn't have to ask me to stay after class; I waited. She walked over to her desk and grabbed the notebook and began to speak but I interrupted her with my insecurities, "I know it's not good. I know it doesn't have a topic sentence and sophisticated words, but I tried. I really tried." My words trailed off into silence because there was nothing else for me to say. I waited for Mrs. Roberts to respond. It seemed endless. She passed me the notebook, and asked me to read it aloud to her, reciting her classroom rule, "Words cannot just be seen, they must be heard." I open my mouth and I read:

> Last night I showered
> trying to get you out of me
> wash out the dirt of you and find myself in the ashes
> scrubbed my skin and I wanted to bleed.
> I wanted to feel pain.
> One harsh enough to cover the bruises,
> you created in my body.
> Forced into me.
> I can still feel you inside my mind.
> GET OUT OF MY HEAD!
> GET OUT OF MY HEAD!
> GET OUT OF MY HEAD!
> You're trying to take over,
> but I can't let you.
> I still don't have the words to stop you.
> I don't know what to say.
> I just want you gone.
> Please get off of my skin.
> Even water, can't take your stench away.
> You took what mattered away.
> YOU STOLE my confidence.
> But you didn't just take that
> you stole so much more.

We stared at each other in silence. Mrs. Roberts came over to me and as she hugged me she replied, "Dywanna, you are a poet." I pushed her away from me and screamed, "I am not a poet! I don't do poetry! I don't understand it and poetry is hard. This isn't hard! This is just truth! This is just me!" She pulled me back into her embrace and said,

> Poetry is pure emotion. You bleed yourself on the page. It does not need topic sentences. It does not need punctuation. It needs to be powerful and raw. You are bearing witness to your own life through your writing. This is what I see. You are a writer. You are a poet.

I did not believe her. It could not be that simple. Poets were artists and I was simply a grifter playing the part of a happy adolescent girl. I continued to write in my notebook, and it became my constant companion – a concrete object manifesting my pain. I would study words trying to make them connect organically. As I read books, I would try to discern how an author compelled me to feel. Time passed, and pages filled, and I needed a new companion. I found a new journal and continued to write. I realize that as I wrote, I was not alone; my truth space was a living presence always with me. She, my poetic muse, was both critical and accepting. She was curious and playful. She was my close confidant and one of the few individuals who saw me in my totality. I could no longer call poetry a thing. She was a person, a radiant individual, and she understood me. I was a poet.

Unbeknownst to me, Mrs. Robert heard my quiet demand for a truth space, and since that time writing has always been cathartic. My pen has been steadfast through a torrid love affair lasting decades. Now my pen is my confidant, my pathway to truth; so much so that I coined an ode of thanks.

> To My Pen:
> You have always loved me.
> I've walked away from you countless times
> and you sit waiting patiently for my return.
> You cast no judgment;
> instead, welcome me
> when I'm vulnerable.
> You've captured a thousand tears
> and transformed them
> into a cathartic ocean.
> You've held my secrets
> tightly bound in your grasp
> until I was ready to speak their truth.
> You've danced to the melody
> of my heartbeat and sang
> soft, lilting lullabies.

> You are wisdom and healing.
> I am my most perfect self
> when I hold you in my fingers.
> How can I thank you for
> loving me so purely?
> You are life.
> Always!

My pen is more than an instrument of communication. It is a tool of comprehension and discernment. Therefore, writing is transformational because writing poetry has become a place to both understand and express life and the research experience which are, for me, one and the same. Thus, in this book, I share my work with five eighth-grade adolescent Black girls and a close examination of our experiences together as we battled the intersections of race, gender, and size. We worked together after school in Houston Middle School's (pseudonym) Media Center for over six weeks. Surrounded by books that sheltered a variety of stories, we bonded and shared our truths. With affirming compassion, we pondered and navigated our own and each other's emotional baggage.

Deeply impacted by my own experiences, I wanted to learn how these young Black girls responded to the discourse used to describe and define obesity and race; were socialized into their beliefs surrounding obesity and race; made meaning of the ideals of obesity, race, gender, and beauty portrayed in media; and interpreted obesity and race in their everyday lives. Together, we explored and documented the creation and impact of an eighth-grade truth space where we responded to depictions of obesity in adolescent literature and media; analyzed societal constructs that often deny particular aspects of adolescent identity; came to understand more about the intersection of obesity, race, and gender in media and our daily lives; and created counternarratives about gender, race, and obesity.

The girls' stories, alongside my reflections, led to insights into the nuances and complexities of truth as we discovered that: (1) Multiple truths can exist side by side; (2) all truths, like all stories, are legitimate and valuable; (3) there are multiple ways of expressing our truths; (4) denying, negating, or ignoring truths is a traumatic and violent act.; (5) sharing our truths, like telling our stories, is a harbinger of healing and liberation; (6) truth-telling, much like love, is rooted in justice; there can be no justice without truth; and (7) the opportunity to analyze texts and create counternarratives nurtured our critical consciousness.

I situate this work alongside other Black Women Scholar/Researchers who are a part of the Black Girl Literacies Collective (BGLC). "The BGLC is a space for resistance and a site for possibility in literacy and English education research, theory, and practice. We are Black women scholars actively committed to bringing research and practice to the forefront, work that calls out and works against educational harm toward Black women and girls, while simultaneously promoting their social and academic success." BGLC sista scholars include Marcelle Haddix, Gholnecsar E. Muhammad, Detra Price-Dennis, Yolanda Sealey-Ruiz, Sherell A. McArthur, Carmen Kynard, Elaine Richardson, Erica Womack, LaToya T. Sawyer, April Baker-Bell, Tonya Perry, Bettina Love, Tamara Butler, Delicia T. Greene, Reba Y. Hodge, Fahima Ife, Maima Chea, Stephanie Jones, Stephanie Toliver, Em Kirkwood, Autumn A. Griffin, and Ebony Elizabeth Thomas.

Reference

Dunbar, P. L. (1969). *Lyrics of lowly life. With an intro. by W. D. Howells.* Arno Press.

2
GEMS OF TRUTH
Research Partners as Love Advocates

odo nyera

Daybreak.
Sunlight softly caresses my cheek,
Ending my slumber.
Instantly, alert I remember
a vengeful world;
one existing outside
love's refuge.
Many fear us
and only want to use our talents
for their profit and gain.
As I searched to find sanctuary
from blinding hatred...
I was overcome.
And then Blackness birthed me.

I thought of you,
rooted me in your heart,
your laughter became my armor
and our memories a shield.
I transformed into a warrior again
and stood tall with eyes
turned toward the sun.
I would fight with you,
for you.
for me,
for our past,

> *through our present.*
> *Together, we will persist and resist.*
> *We will thrive in love*
> *until forever comes.*
>
> ~Dywanna Smith, 2020

I am excited to introduce readers to the five young ladies who dramatically altered my life through our critical literacy explorations. These young women, who affectionately coined themselves the Blue Diamonds, were my research partners; but in truth, they are much more. Through their bodies, stories, courage, and intellect, the young women are love advocates (Garnett, 2017). Freire and Macedo (1987) suggested that critical literacy should engage students in developing a critical consciousness which they use to probe the interrelated structures in which they come to know and learn the world around them. Such an analysis moves students from solely consuming information to being socio-politically aware and capable of speaking back to injustice. Developing a sense of critical consciousness is also an underlying principle of Critical Race Theory (CRT) and Black Feminist Thought (Collins, 2000; Ladson-Billings, 1995) (discussed in Chapter 4), two frames for thinking that are foundational to my work. Using these constructs to frame my research and recalibrate my vision, I utilize the labels *research partner* and *love advocate* to reflect my commitment to anchoring this study in what I hope to establish as a culture of reciprocal knowledge construction and love. I learned from my research partners just as they learned from my contributions. As research partners, they helped me collect, analyze, and decide how to write about data. As love advocates, they exemplified, courage, fortitude, and resilience. By communing in our truth space, we all became more critically conscious and deepened our notions of love.

The love we shared and communicate is a Radical Black love that centers the heart, moving beyond the eurocentric and white supremacist notion that learning begins with the brain. Our definition of learning, therefore, wholeheartedly rejects Descartes' notion of "I think, therefore, I am" which makes learning an individualistic and isolationist task. Instead, this work is rooted, as I am, in the African notion of Ubuntu: I am because we are. Ubuntu means recognizing, internalizing, and legitimizing humanity in its vast permutations. In this manner, learning does not begin with the brain. Instead, it is a communion that starts with the heart and ultimately blends the heart, mind, and spirit. Ubuntu tells us as educators that if we want our students to achieve academic success, we must connect our hearts to that of our students.

Aligned with this view of love, my work is also grounded in the view that, for educators to heal and transform our world, we must engage our inner selves in soul-speak, a complex raw and honest dialogue grounded in agape love (Dillard, 2012; Evans-Winters, 2019; Smith, 2018). Agape love is immeasurable and incomparable. It is a love of goodwill, faithfulness, and commitment. Soul

Speak is but one of the manifestations of this kind of love and, therefore, one of the many ways to counter the spirit murders of Black girls that routinely occur in public school classrooms. Soul Speak demands an environment of mutual love and respect (Love, 2019; Smith, Kelly-Morris, & Chapman, 2021). This was central to my relationship with the Blue Diamonds.

It is with these notions of Ubuntu and Soul Speak that I also define and perceive Black Girlhood. Although our particular truth space was comprised of ladies who each identified as cisgender, it would be disingenuous and dehumanizing to limit Black Girlhood to a singular definition. Black Girlhood manifests itself in many ways: cisgender, queer, transgender, and non-binary. All forms must be valued, but even more, all forms deserve unapologetic and radical love. To all the Black girls of the world ... I see you. I know you. I love you. I am because we are.

While I recognize that the issue of obesity is far-reaching affecting all races, my work to understand truth spaces focused on African American girls because it was my own tumultuous journey through adolescence as a Black girl, and my concern with former Black students struggling to deal with assault in and out of school around issues of obesity, race, and gender which sparked the inquiry. The research partners were from a range of socioeconomic backgrounds. They also comprised a variety of body sizes. This is because our understanding of body size does not occur with obese individuals alone. We utilize the knowledge of both thin and that which is not thin to formulate perception. It is the constant tension between the obese body and the "thin ideal" where knowledge construction is formed (Bordo, 1993; Cox, 2020; Taylor, 2018).

All members of the group were eighth-grade students. I sought research partners from the oldest students in the middle school because I planned to utilize texts that were not appropriate for younger audiences – movies with PG-13 ratings, musical excerpts with explicit lyrics such as profane words, and young adult novels that were rated by the American Library Association to be appropriate for eighth-graders. Since these criteria yielded a large result of possible partners, I identified the partners by interviewing Houston Middle School's afterschool coordinator and teachers using what is called "snowballing sampling" (Patton, 2001, p. 243) or identifying participants by talking to people who know them to determine who, from their perspective, might provide the richest information. As a result, I determined the five students who became partners in the study.

The research partners were members of the Houston school's afterschool program. The afterschool program hosted students in grades six to eight. The program services students who have not met mastery of specific literacy and mathematics skills according to the state's assessment system. The program was also developed to meet Raven School District's six identified purposes for academic improvement: tutorials, homework assistance, childcare, compensatory remediation, enrichment, and test preparation. The goal of the afterschool program was to provide a haven for students to engage in structured activities that would benefit them academically, emotionally, and physically. Since the love advocates had been part of this program for their entire middle school experience, there was already a strong established community among them. Having taught previously at the school, when I became a full-time graduate student, I continued my association with Houston by supervising student teachers and serving as the school's liaison to the university providing professional development for Houston teachers. Thus, I had the pleasure of interacting with students in the afterschool program before the initiation of this study.

As I neared the time to disseminate this work, each of the group members selected a personal pseudonym. Using their pseudonyms, I introduce the six of us below.

Amir

Amir was well-known throughout Houston Middle School for her dynamic personality. She could often be heard shouting from one end of the hallway to the next enthusiastically greeting her friends. Amir was a year behind the other Blue Diamond girls as she had been retained during her seventh-grade year. Amir and I already knew each other as we met when I observed her seventh-grade English/language arts class. Amir was energetic, loved track and talking on her cellphone.

Marie

At first shy, Marie opened and began discussing other interests such as music and cooking. As she did, I realized, Marie had an infectious smile. She was an avid reader and could often be seen in the media center. Consultation with the after-school coordinator revealed that Marie had never completed an entire school term due to suspensions or expulsions.

Jennifer

I met Jennifer when she was in the sixth grade and I was a guest speaker in her English/language arts class. Because of her energy and charisma, people were drawn to Jennifer. It was not shocking that during the lesson, Jennifer could constantly be observed turning around in her seat and talking to her classmates. Although it frustrated her teacher, I wanted to build upon her gregarious nature. When I was the guest teacher for her class, I modified Jennifer's writing assignment, asking her to describe her ideas orally and then put them on paper. The class time elapsed and Jennifer was still writing. She called herself a writer in progress.

Kelsey

Kelsey and I met for the first time during the fall semester of 2013. She typically always smiled and could be observed mediating arguments between her friends. She was a technology junkie and would easily describe how to use social media. She loved music, dance, and of course, boys. I quickly learned that Kelsey was an apt caregiver. She checked on each of us throughout our commune in the truth space. She usually greeted us with a "You good?" An expression to see if we were emotional, mentally, and physically well. One could not hide with Kelsey; she had a keen ability to peer into your eyes and find your truth. She possessed, as my grandmother would say, an old soul.

Melody

Melody and I also met for the first time during the fall semester of 2013. Melody was a member of the poetry club which I helped sponsor as a liaison and I had the pleasure of reading her work. We bonded over poetry's ability to speak for us. Melody was quite reserved and often did not talk in her classes. She did, however, speak loudly through her poetry. She would spend hours writing and sharing her poems with friends via text messages. When she was not writing; she also read fanfiction on popular cellphone apps. She loved music, videos, and fashion and often shifted through magazines. She did not, however, consider those activities a form of reading.

Dywanna

I am Dywanna. At the time of this work, I identified as a researcher, scholar, and middle school educator with 12 years of middle level experience. I taught English/language arts within Houston Middle School until I decided to become a full-time student to pursue my doctoral degree. I am an avid reader and writer who claims poetry as my heart's language and self-identifies as being fat; a moniker that has served various roles within my life including shame, depression, and finally a loving acceptance.

Becoming Blue Diamonds

During the first of our six meetings, the research partners decided that our truth space needed a name. They tossed out and discarded suggestions. Jennifer suggested the name blue devils as this was the mascot of the high school in which they all would attend. Kelsey suggested dropping the name devils as it had a negative connotation and emphasized, "We ain't devils anyway. We good. We shine like diamonds." Marie exclaimed, "That's it! That's it right there!" As a group, the research partners voted and all agreed on the name, and the Blue Diamonds were formed.

My role was initially an observer/facilitator (Creswell & Creswell, 2018). Although I was living and had lived the very experiences we would explore, I could not assume that I was a Blue Diamond; this right could only be obtained through invitation. So, rather than imposing myself as a Blue Diamond, I joined in as seamlessly as possible, while recognizing that they would always see me as a teacher and in some ways, an other: I listened to discussions, shared my journal as they shared theirs, assisted with homework, and celebrated academic successes. When the girls discussed family drama, I did not judge. Instead, I shared examples from my family's saga. On day three, the girls were hugging goodbye. I sat back and observed the support and love. Suddenly, Melody looked at me and proclaimed, "Why ain't you in this?" I did not know what to reply. Kelsey sensed my confusion and stated, "You supposed to be a part of this hug. You know you a Blue Diamond too."

Getting to the Heart of the Matter

This study matters. It matters for teachers, teacher educators, administrators but most importantly, it matters in the lives of Black girls everywhere whose voices are unheard, demeaned, and dismissed. First, this work centered on the convergence of race, gender, and size, has the potential to fill gaps in the literature because little work exists that examines robust accounts of these converging social identities as articulated by adolescent Black girls. Second, the study examined the use of critical theories to support eighth-grade girls in analyzing the body as a textual artifact, also a gap in the literature and educators' knowledge. While traditional texts, digital texts, and a range of other texts are often analyzed critically by middle school students, there is a paucity of studies focusing on students' examination of the body as text. The study also analyzed the ideology surrounding obesity through the eyes of five young women and myself, a form of analysis rarely found in current literature used to inform educators. Finally, this work potentially broadens knowledge in the field by offering strategies for changing schools as reproducers of societal inequities to become places of critical inquiry and examiners of dominant narratives about obesity, race, and gender.

Normalization of the Thin, White Female Form

The normalization and reification of the thin, white girl/woman's form have existed for centuries. The objectification of women no matter their race has long made us susceptible to acts of violence, not always with traditional weapons, but with the discourse, we use to describe young women (Kilbourne, 2012). To compound this complex matter, the white race has been normalized and because of the permanence of racism, also known as racial realism (Bell, 1992), the white girl form will always be idealized (Crenshaw, 1991). For many, the idea of racial realism or the fact that racism will always be a permanent factor in social, political, financial, health, and in this case educational spaces, may be distressing. Yet, this nuanced perspective displays how, as Black girls and women, we are subject to both racism and society's brutal objectification (LaVoulle & Ellison, 2017). Additionally, social constructionists argue that, just as with race, body size – thinness in particular – is a normalized social construct (Cox, 2020). Barak (1998) declared, "There are no purely objective definitions; all definitions are value-laden and biased to some degree," (p. 21) and so biases about size unveil additional layers of weight stigma and discrimination. If an individual does not achieve these visions of constructed normality; they are ostracized and ridiculed (Cox, 2020; Taylor, 2018).

This idea of the white and thin form as normal is depicted in novels, music, and movies and stands in marked contrast to depictions of the obese, fat, or overweight form (Kilbourne, 2012). Cahnman (1968) contended in a society that perpetually emphasizes beauty as status, being obese or overweight disgraces the individual and tarnishes physical appearance. Many social theorists further argue that the labels "overweight" and "obese" only serve to marginalize certain individuals in our society (Cox, 2020; Oliver, 2006; Rothblum & Solovay, 2009). These labels, when internalized, signify the need to lose weight for personal and social acceptance (Cox, 2020; Taylor, 2018). When understanding these realities in the lives of women in conjunction with the permanence of racism and how it operates within American society (Bell, 1992; Delgado, Stefancic, & Harris, 2017), it is easy to see how obese African American girls experience inequitable practices and institutional racism conflated with sizism on many levels.

This study created a contested space for African American adolescent girls to speak their truths about these intersecting identity factors, which allowed them to confess past trauma, analyze and critique dominant narratives, and narrate new understandings. Johnson (2014) described the contested space as

> a site of cultural, racial, and ethnic struggle; therefore, this space is not perfectly harmonious or a space of ease. Contested spaces can become a tool that pushes people to learn, expand understanding, take a new perspective, and stretch awareness
>
> (p. 132)

A contested space examines inequitable power distribution by analyzing historical and contemporary examples simultaneously which allows a multi-level examination of oppressive power constructs (Baszile, 2013). As a result of the contested spaces created through our truth space, this study offers richer and more robust stories than currently exist in the education field which largely neglects the inclusion and examination of young women's views and experiences concerning the intersection of race, size, and gender.

Engaging Adolescents in Critically Examining the Body as Text

Cox (2020) contended fat or obese bodies are read as lazy, lacking moral fortitude, a willing transgression of an established boundary. Similarly, Murray (2005) stated:

> We exist in a culture of negative collective "knowingness" about fatness. As members of Western society, we presume we know the histories of all bodies, particularly those of fat women; we believe we know their desires (which must be out of control) and their will (which must be weak.) We read a fat body on the street and believe we "know" its truth.
>
> (p. 154)

This "presumed knowing" leads to a politicized stigma for obese or overweight individuals (Hynnä & Kryola, 2019; Patterson-Faye, 2018; Taylor, 2018) and a narrow monolithic reading of the body as text. This becomes a normalized reading, as the reader draws on society's messages to filter through information, lenses, and stances; constantly re-envisioning and reinterpreting a text. However, guiding students to use critical theory (or a critical lens) to examine the body as text (as well as other texts), has the potential to allow the obese frame to be reimagined as beautiful, healthy, and worthy of validation (Cox, 2020; Hynnä & Kryola, 2019; Taylor, 2018). Through this multifaceted process, students can go beyond superficial residuals; begin to question and challenge obesity and find new meaning; thereby resisting traditional educational approaches which restrict the analysis and discussion of any text and deny critical and reflective thinking (Butler, 2017; Gordan, Dukes, & Muhammad, 2019; Muhammad & Haddix, 2016; Price-Dennis, 2016; Sealey-Ruiz, 2016). It is, for this reason, I believe classrooms should always employ critical literacy learning which encompasses social, political, and historical contexts and allows students to closely examine the influence of societal establishments on their everyday lives (Hynnä & Kryola, 2019; Patterson-Faye, 2016; Williams, 2017).

Grounded in these convictions, my study created spaces for and examined the process of how adolescent girls used critical theories to examine the body as text within the wider examination of social representations of race, gender, and size. Not only did they examine these issues critically, but our truth space provided unconditional support for them to speak back to those issues – an important element of critical work.

In using this framework which places the body as text at its center, this study pushes the boundaries of existing research as students and teachers work to unmask and disrupt practices in oral, written, and popular culture. Students need to critically analyze texts such as young adolescent literature, social media, and/or music videos (McArthur, 2016) with a specific focus on the inter-relationship between size, race, and gender (Butler, 2017; Gordan et al., 2019). Drawing from critical theories that emphasize power, privilege, and empowerment (Price-Dennis, Muhammad, McArthur, & Haddix, 2017), students and teachers worked collaboratively to critique dominant social practices through oppositional and resistant readings of the text (Apple, 1982; Baker-Bell, Stanbrough, & Everett, 2017). In ways rarely seen in studies of adolescents, I hope that this research will broaden notions of what counts as text which can be read critically, and thereby provide models for ways adolescents can be supported in tackling school and community issues (Baker-Bell, Butler, & Johnson, 2017).

Analyzing Obesity Ideology

Simply put, ideology is a set of ideas and doctrines which when combined create a distinct perspective of a social group; it is an essential component in maintaining domination of one group over another (Marx, Engels, & Hobsbawm, 1996). Gee (2015) noted Marx's belief that human beings' ideologies are a result of interacting with their physical and social environments and further postulated that societies have been created to ensure power and privilege for a few elites.

When considering obesity, ideology is paramount in the medical profession, for example, the ever-changing definitions of "health" that have occurred during the 20th century. Oliver (2006) contended over the past two decades, select scientists, doctors, and health officials have:

> actively campaigned to define our growing weight as an epidemic. They have created a very low definition of what is "overweight" and "obese" so that tens of millions of Americans including archetypes such as basketball star Michael Jordon are now considered to weigh too much. And, most importantly, they have established bodyweight as a barometer of wellness, so that being thin is equated with being healthy.
>
> (p. 5)

This creation of polarizing dynamics, those who are thin and therefore healthy, and those who are obese and therefore unhealthy, establishes an ideology that provides criteria and definitions for who is allowed to fully participate in society and who must be marginalized (Cox, 2020; Patterson-Faye, 2016). It also establishes a net worth for the body because a thin frame is more commercially profitable than an obese frame (LaVoulle & Ellison, 2017). Fat people can be terminated or suspended because of their weight, despite good job performance (Reece, 2018; The Bronfenbrenner Center for Translational Research (BCTR), 2019). In one study, reviewers found that 5.7% of individuals at normal weight felt they experienced discrimination in contrast to 19.2% for people considered overweight and 41.8% for those considered obese (The Bronfenbrenner Center for Translational Research (BCTR), 2019).

More frightening is research which documents that negative attitudes start in preschool and progress as students age (Pont, Puhl, Cook, & Slusser, 2017). Addressing those alarming realities, this critical study created sorely needed alternative pathways to self-actualization and body image acceptance by unapologetically confronting obesity ideology and challenging the perceived wisdom of obesity ideology through the creation of counternarratives. It also allows for, as Freire (2000) stated, space for stakeholders to tell their stories of injustice: the bullying, teasing, and violence experienced because of size providing cathartic healing and allowing research partners to expose, critique, and challenge the master narrative. Engaging in this study revealed the extent to which obesity ideology operates in conjunction with other systems of power and privilege in the lives of a small group of adolescent girls. By deeply analyzing such constructs, research partners became empowered and informed activists who help to dismantle the harmful effects of this ideology.

Schools as Critical Consumers of Societal Inequities Around Weight

For many adolescent girls, body weight can be a complicated and sometimes multifaceted issue because if there is no space in schools or classrooms for learning to critically analyze messages they receive about their bodies; educational institutions become reproducers of social inequities. This study sought to change that reality by supporting students in critically analyzing messages about body size including those that emphasize and even at times reward fat-shaming (Pont et al., 2017). Consider the successful reality series *The Biggest Loser* in which obese contestants battle to see which one can lose the most weight over a weeklong period. The show's climactic moment is always the weekly weigh-in where contestants stand on a massive scale displaying their weekly weight loss. Ultimately, the winner of *The Biggest Loser* challenge receives a cash prize and the praises of coaches, trainers, family members, and friends adoring their new thinner frame. Health statistics, however, are never shared. Implications are that simply losing weight, makes a person healthier even if the extreme workouts and intense dietary restrictions can further injure the body and cause physical and psychological illness.

Viewers are so immersed in the grueling exercise programs and motivational speeches; they never seem to consider the duality of the show's name. Honestly, I did not ponder this subject long myself until a former seventh-grade student discussed how she considered the show to be rude and thought it should immediately be removed from the weekly line-up. When I inquired as to why she held staunchly to this belief, she quickly rolled her eyes and said, "Come on, Ms. Smith!" She used her forefinger and thumb to form an "L" and placed it on her forehead. "That show says you are not just losing weight; you are going to lose your loser status as well. It's really a joke." Her astute observation aligns with contestant testimonies. Kai Hibbard, a *Biggest Loser* contestant in 2006, lost 121 pounds and ridiculed the show because fat-shaming was paramount. She reflected on how trainers would tell contestants, "You're going to die before your children grow up"; "You're going to die, just like your mother"; and "We've picked out your fat-person coffin" (Marr, 2015). These insensitive remarks were to be an inspiration to drop the dreaded and evil weight; but also serve to reinforce the notion to be obese is to be relegated to the margins of society (Cox, 2020; Hynnä & Kryola, 2019; Taylor, 2018).

Though the contestants may be the source of shaming, they are praised for eradicating their fat, but why? Being thin is not synonymous with better health; just as being overweight is not synonymous with poor health (Cox, 2020; Oliver, 2006). Yet, our adolescent girls often experience pressure to conform to normative ideals that equate being thin with being healthy and beautiful, and obese as being unhealthily worthy of ridicule and derision (Patterson-Faye, 2016). The decision, however, to adopt or reject the thin-as-healthy-and-beautiful ideal is dependent upon experiences with size and body ideals in the contexts of their lives (Cox, 2020; Patterson-Faye, 2016; Taylor, 2018). Because schools are often sites of transformation or reproducers of the dominant ideology, I was led to examine possibilities for the role of educational institutions in interrupting marginalizing ideologies.

Ironically, the role of schools as critical sites to examine and interrogate body image, obesity, fat-shaming, and ultimately fat-acceptance has little been explored in qualitative literature. Mueller, Pearson, Muller, Frank, & Turner (2010) maintained that schools blend

> developmentally-similar adolescents for long periods provide a social context that is ripe for observation, judgment, and social comparison. The foods girls eat, size of their bodies, weight values and behaviors they verbally or visibly endorse, and their appearance can be observed and used to judge.
>
> (p. 65)

Because schools are instrumental in socializing adolescent girls, it is crucial to examine the role schools play in creating weight-related cultural values (Cox, 2020; Patterson-Faye, 2016; Taylor, 2018). Equally important is to examine how schools can become sites of resistance to hegemony, particularly about singular definitions of beauty, size, and health. Resistance to these dominant definitions can only be achieved by critically examining the fear and hatred surrounding the obese frame (Cox, 2020; Patterson-Faye, 2016; Taylor, 2018). This takes a critically courageous stance rarely exhibited in curriculum and the professional literature.

Freire described courage as a state of being characterized by action "in spite of" fear (Freire, 2000). For him, courage and fear are alternating sides of the same coin; one cannot exist without the other. The only way to begin controlling the fear that binds is to educate it (Freire, 2000). If schools are to be transformational catalysts, adolescent girls need contested spaces to explore the curiosities and fears regarding obesity. Classrooms must become dialogic spaces where students are buffered from emotional turmoil, encouraged to hear, analyze, and interpret alternative points of view – a critical space which fosters a new way of "knowing" and validating the obese body (Baker-Bell, Stanbrough, & Everett, 2017; Patterson-Faye, 2016; Price-Dennis et al., 2017; Smith, 2018). It is this criticality and focus on the need for change in schools that mark the heart of our truth space.

Finding Sanctuary in Truth: Research as an Act of Love

I began this inquiry because I was wounded and saw that students around me were wounded as well. I knew that schooling could be a better place in support of young Black women who were negotiating intersections of race, gender, and size. So, I sought insight from the experts: Black adolescent girls. I not only found wisdom; I, like them, found sanctuary in truth spaces. We were all hesitant in sharing our stories, but collectively we realized, we were not alone; and speaking our stories, gave us power. As I think about the experiences of Black girls throughout this nation, I realize truth spaces are vital for resilience, rejuvenation, and revitalizing education. Through this study, I opened my soul and my stories to five adolescent girls. I realized, it is our stories that will lead to understanding; it is our stories that will lead to healing; it is our stories that will restore and rebuild; it is our stories that will lead to transformation. May it inspire you to adopt truth spaces as a loving pedagogical practice in your work to become transformational warrior activists. Once again, I use my pen and my words as a lens to analyze and interpret the world and as an offering to teachers who have the power to make a difference in the lives of students most oppressed.

References

Apple, M. W. (1982). *Education and power*. Routledge & Kegan Paul.
Baker-Bell, A., Butler, T., & Johnson, L. L. (2017). 116 English Education, V49 N2, January 2017 English Education, January 2017 The pain and the wounds: A call for critical race english education in the wake of racial violence. *English Education, 49*(2), 117–129.
Baker-Bell, A., Stanbrough, R., & Everett, S. (2017). The stories they tell: Mainstream media, pedagogies of healing, and critical media literacy. *English Education, 49*(2), 130–152.
Barak, G. (1998). *Integrating criminologies*. Allyn and Bacon.
Baszile, D. T. (2013). Who does she think she is: Growing up nationalist and ending up teaching race in White space. *Journal of Curriculum Theorizing, 19*(3), 25–38.
Bell, D. (1992). *Faces at the bottom of the well: The permanence of racism*. Basic Books.
Bordo, S. (1993). *Unbearable weight: Feminism, Western culture, and the body*. University of California Press.

Butler, T. (2017). #Say [ing] her name as critical demand: English education in the age of erasure. *English Education, 49*(2), 153–178.

Cahnman, W. (1968). The stigma of obesity. *The Sociological Quarterly, 93*(3), 283–299.

Collins, P. H. (2000). *Black feminist thought: Knowledge, consciousness, and the politics of empowerment*. Routledge.

Cox, J. (2020). *Fat girls in black bodies: Creating communities of our own*. North Atlantic Books.

Crenshaw, K. (1991). Mapping the margins: Intersectionality, identity politics, and violence against women of color. *Stanford Law Review, 43*(6), 1241–1299.

Creswell, J. W., & Creswell, J. D. (2018). *Research design: Qualitative, quantitative, and mixed methods approaches* (5th ed.). SAGE.

Delgado, R., Stefancic, J., & Harris, A. P. (2017). *Critical race theory: An introduction*. New York University Press.

Dillard, C. (2012). *Learning to (Re) member the things we've learned to forget: Endarkened feminisms, spirituality, and the sacred nature of research and teaching (black studies and critical thinking)* 1st printing edition by Dillard, Cynthia B. (2012) Paperback (1st printing edition). Peter Lang Publishing Inc.

Evans-Winters, V. E. (2019). *Black feminism in qualitative inquiry: A mosaic for writing our daughter's body (futures of data analysis in qualitative research)* (1st ed.). Routledge.

Freire, P. (2000). *Pedagogy of the oppressed*. Continuum.

Freire, P., & Macedo, D. P. (1987). *Literacy: Reading the word and the world*. Bergin & Garvey.

Garnett, J. (2017). Love is a parable. Retrieved 2020, from https://loveisaparable.com/

Gee, J. P. (2015). *Social linguistics and literacies: Ideology in discourses*. Routledge.

Gordan, C., Dukes, N., & Muhammad, G. (2019). Defying the single narrative of black girls' literacies: A narrative inquiry exploring an African American read-in. *Multicultural Perspectives, 21*(1), 3–10.

Hynnä, K., & Kryola, K. (2019). "Feel in Your Body": Fat activist affects in blogs. *Social Media Society, 5*(4), 2056305119879983.

Johnson, L. L. (2014). Who let the elephant in the room? Analyzing race and racism through a critical family literacy book club. (Doctoral dissertation, University of South Carolina) [Abstract]. Retrieved from http://scholarcommons.sc.edu/etd/3048

Kilbourne, J. (2012). *Can't buy my love: How advertising changes the way we think and feel*. Simon & Schuster.

Ladson-Billings, G. (1995). But that's just good teaching! The case for culturally relevant pedagogy. *Theory into Practice, 34*(3), 159–165.

LaVoulle, C., & Ellison, T. (2017). The bad bitch barbie craze and beyoncé: African American women's bodies as commodities in hip-hop culture, images, and media. *Taboo: The Journal of Culture and Education, 16*(2), 7.

Love, B. (2019). *We want to do more than survive: Abolitionist teaching and the pursuit of educational freedom* (Illustrated ed.). Beacon Press.

Marr, M. (2015, January). Biggest loser' contestant: Show a 'fat-shaming disaster. *Miami Herald*. Retrieved from http://www.miamiherald.com/entertainment/celebrities/article7584338.html

Marx, K., Engels, F., & Hobsbawm, E. J. (1996). *The Communist manifesto: A modern edition*. Verso.

McArthur, S. (2016). Black girls and critical media literacy for social activism. *English Education, 48*(4), 462–479.

Mueller, A. S., Pearson, J., Muller, C., Frank, K., & Turner, A. (2010). Sizing up peers: Adolescent girls' weight control and social comparison in the school context. *Journal of Health and Social Behavior, 51*(1), 64–78.

Muhammad, G., & Haddix, M. (2016). Centering Black girls' ways of knowing: A historical review of literature on the multiple literacies of Black girls, English Education. *English Education, 48*(4), 299–336.

Murray, S. (2005). (Un/Be) coming out? Rethinking fat politics. *Social Semiotics, 15*(2), 153–163.

Oliver, J. E. (2006). *Fat politics: The real story behind America's obesity epidemic.* Oxford University Press.

Patterson-Faye, C. (2016). I like the way you move': Theorizing fat, black and sexy. *Sexualities, 19*(8), 926–944.

Patterson-Faye, C. F. (2018). When and where I always enter: An auto-ethnographic approach to black women's body size politics in academia. In M. A. Hunter (Ed.), *The new black sociologists: Historical and contemporary perspectives* (pp. 89–100). Routledge.

Patton, M. Q. (2001). *Qualitative research and evaluation methods.* Sage Publications.

Pont, S. J., Puhl, R., Cook, S. R., & Slusser, W. (2017). Stigma experienced by children and adolescents with obesity. *Pediatrics, 140*(6), 1–13. doi:10.1542/peds.2017-3034

Price-Dennis, D. (2016). Developing curriculum to support black girls' literacies in digital spaces. *English Education, 48*(4), 337–361.

Price-Dennis, D., Muhammad, G., McArthur, S., & Haddix, M. (2017). The multiple identities and literacies of Black girlhood: A conversation about creating spaces for Black girl voices. *Journal of Language and Literacy Education, 13*(2), 1–18.

Reece, R. (2018). Coloring weight stigma: On race, colorism, weight stigma, and the failure of additive intersectionality. *Sociology of Race and Ethnicity, 5*(3), 388–400.

Rothblum, E. D., & Solovay, S. (2009). *The fat studies reader.* New York University Press.

Sealey-Ruiz, Y. (2016). Why black girls' literacies matter: New literacies for a new era. *English Education, 48*(3), 290–298.

Smith, D. (2018). Telling our stories; sharing our lives: storytelling as the heart of resistance. In L. L. Johnson, G. Boutte, & G. Greene (Eds.), *African diaspora literacy: The heart of transformation in K–12 schools and teacher education African diaspora literacy: The heart of transformation in K–12 schools and teacher education* (pp. 107–125). Lexington Books, an Imprint of The Rowman & Littlefield Publishing Group.

Smith, D., Kelly-Morris, K., & Chapman, S. (2021). (Re)Membering: Black women engaging memory through journaling. *Urban Education,* 004208592110039. doi:10.1177/00420859211003932

Taylor, S. R. (2018). *The body is not an apology: The power of radical self-love.* Berrett-Koehler.

The Bronfenbrenner Center for Translational Research (BCTR). (2019, July 09). The growing problem of weight discrimination. Retrieved from https://www.psychologytoday.com/us/blog/evidence-based-living/201907/the-growing-problem-weight-discrimination

Williams, A. (2017). Fat people of color: Emergent intersectional discourse online. *Social Sciences, 6*(15), 1–16.

3
FAKE LOVE

The Truth Behind the Caring Myth

odo nyera

False Offerings
You come to me
offering empty condolences
Words quickly uttered which
bypassed your heart before
falling haphazardly at my feet.
…And you expect me… to what?
Be grateful?
Be pleased?
Offer forgiveness?
What exactly do you want from me?
You hunt my children.
Crack open their earth-born bodies.
Leave me repeatedly broken.
I've buried my children,
while you lined your pockets,
with our ingenuity.
As I grieved, you sit drinking tea.
Unbothered, your lives moved on.
Not for me.
Each time it happens.
Every time you snatch a life
from the divine
time stands still;
and I…
I am left breathless.

*I simply cannot breathe
because reality is a mountain
on my chest.
And you think
thoughts and prayers
are enough?
You type fake
outrage on
social media
like 280 characters
can capture
their essence.
While, I...
I am counting
heartbeats to prove
I am not the walking dead.
But back to you.
Do you feel better?
Have you patted
yourself on the back?
Posted your fake love
so, an adoring public
will proclaim, "Well-done?"
Cleansed your spirit
with good intentions?
You gain status by
brutalizing Black bodies.
I want nothing from you.
Your words are barren.
Wait!
No... that is not right.
I do want something.
I demand something from you.
I want your sacrifice.
I want you to cast
your white privilege
and white supremacy
at my feet;
so I can set fire
to them and rebuild anew.
I want the flames to dance
to the heavens.
I want it to burn so bright...*

Fake Love

> *so luminescent*
> *That Sandra*
> *That Ahmaud*
> *That Atatiana*
> *That Tamir*
> *That Yvonne*
> *That Breonna*
> *That Ma'Khia*
> *will send their tears*
> *in a river to flood*
> *this nation.*
> *Purging hatred from your hearts and minds.*
> *Only then will you know*
> *the depths of true love.*
> *I do not think I am asking too much*
> *considering my children's*
> *blood permeates the very ground*
> *we stand upon.*
> *So… no!*
> *I will not absolve your complicit nature,*
> *nor your loveless actions.*
> *No.*
> *I will not accept your thin love.*
> *You will not soothe my rage with*
> *your false offerings.*
> *It*
> *Will*
> *Never*
> *Be*
> *Enough.*
>
> ~Dywanna Smith, 2020

It seems surreal that I am writing a chapter about fake love as America grapples with the realities of the Coronavirus Pandemic. 2020 and 2021 have been years of intense changes and a reminder that some things will never change. I am writing when stay-at-home mandates simultaneously exist alongside a Black woman being shot in her home. I am writing in memory of Honestie Hodges, a beautiful Black girl who at age 11 was wrongfully and brutally handcuffed by police officers, succumbed to Covid-19 complications, at age 14 – illustrating that Black girls and women are fighting to protect their physical, mental, and emotional health, and at the same time, battling racism. I am writing at a time when Black students are being asked to go to schools separated by partitions, unable to touch their friends, and unable to see themselves in the faces of their teachers or in the pages of literature they read. I am writing at a time when grief for losing family members exists besides my struggle to secure freedom for myself, my students, my family, and my world. Though now an assistant professor at Claflin University, a historically Black university founded in 1869, I am still experiencing and bearing witness to the hypervisibility, hypervulnerability, and hypoprotective state which underscores the lives of Black girls and women in America.

Ironically, America's response to Covid-19, particularly when it comes to Black America, illustrates its tenuous relationship with the truth. The stay-at-home orders given by South Carolina's Governor Henry McMasters (Executive Order No. 2020–21, 2020) on March 16, 2020, left me reeling with emotions; but the one which constantly resonated was fear. The solitude erased events which I often used to postpone dealing with my truth: my ongoing battle with depression. My hour-long morning commute was truncated to walking downstairs to my office to begin work. I no longer heard the laughter and voices of my pre-service teachers energizing my spirit. As my campus was now fully virtual, I did not have eager students sitting in my office discussing their fears or dreams. I could not use our conversations to promote young adult literature. The orchestra of sounds which were the voices, music playing from phones, raucous laughter, and clicks of keyboard strokes were now silenced. I felt utterly alone.

To delay the inevitable, I surrounded myself with affirmations. On my bedroom mirror in bold orange marker were the words resume, restore, revive, and repeat; a mantra that was to guide my self-love and focus introspection. I had good intentions, but as Milner & Laughter (2014) stated, good intentions are not enough to produce criticality or sustain a critical consciousness. My isolation placed me in battle with certain truths, and I was reluctant to face them. Yet, truths cannot be tossed aside or hidden. They just lay dormant waiting to be noticed, discussed, and internalized. I realized at this moment, I needed to confess my fear because it debilitates, and forces love to the cursory of our minds. Love demands great risks and profound courage (hooks, 2000; Johnson et al., 2018; Kinloch, 2018; Moore, 2018; Rosenfelt, 2019). Because I know the racially inequitable system is fertile ground for Covid-19 to wreak havoc, I was terrified of loss. I was afraid of losing a student. I was afraid of family and friends dying. Even more so, I was anxious about being isolated with just my thoughts... in the very beginning.

As the days and news headlines began to pass, I found myself settling into a different routine: a new pandemic normal. Resiliently, I cobbled together blessings during the storm: time to write, time to further enjoy family, and time to restore. I had come to some notion of peace: a peace which stood in stark comparison to many of white educator colleagues. As I perused social media, I read their anger because they felt overlooked and their pleas for help with school reopenings being unheard. I felt their rage as they wrote politicians demanding their careers and humanity be recognized and respected. I watched videos where white educators proclaimed themselves essential workers and not expendable ... and

I wholeheartedly agreed with all their sentiments. Yet, I still wondered why they considered America's response to pandemic so shocking … and the reality hit me. For many, this was the first time; their country viewed their lives only as a means for capitalistic gains. Perhaps, for the first time, they were villainized by the same oppressive forces they had complicity ignored.

Fake Love in a White Supremacist Society

Being a Black girl and woman in America had long prepared me for America's "thin love," which as Sethe proclaims in Morrison's *Beloved* (1987), "ain't love at all" (p. 164). America has always ignored me. America overlooked me when I was sexually assaulted because cultures of toxic masculinity and rape are paramount. America ignored my cries for equity in education when my public predominantly Black low-income high school was dilapidated and only offer two advanced placement classes. It turned its back on me as I watched cops target and bully Black kids near my school for supposedly loitering but ignoring the white boys who smoked under trees and catcalled the Black girls. America only recognized me when I could serve as a trope to the myths of meritocracy. America only wanted my talents … not my language, my stories, my skin, or my life. This repeated pattern of denigration, brutality, and misogyny impacting Black girls and women has always been America's standard operating procedure.

Much like Katherine Johnson, Dorothy Vaughn, and Mary Jackson, I was never hidden. As Black girls and women, we exist/ed/s/ing in plain sight. America simply flat-out refuse/ed/s/ing to see us. My use of verb conjugation is strategic and purposeful to demonstrate that America's relationship with Black girls and women was born in violence and it has always turned a blind eye to our physical, emotional, spiritual safety and well-being (Evans-Winters, 2011; Love, 2020; Morris, 2019; Smith, 2016; Winn, 2011). In 1807, when importing enslaved Africans was banned, American slave owners used rape or forced "breeding" to create more human property (DeGruy, 2005) as

> law supported that approach, and … rules of descent and inheritance were changed so that white slave holders could produce as many children through rape as they would like without having to worry about claims upon inheritance produced by the brutal action.
>
> (Jacobs, 2017, p. 45)

America had little concern for Black girls and women when Dr. James Marion Simms forcibly performed gynecological experiments on them (Benia, 2018). America remained blissfully and intentionally silent in 1963, until Addie Mae Collins (14), Cynthia Wesley (14), Carole Robertson (14), and Denise McNair (12) were killed in the 16th Street Baptist Church Bombing (Raines, 1983). America still proclaimed unaware in 2019, when Atatiana Jefferson was murdered in her home by police officers (Ortiz, 2019a). America's legacy of sexual, emotional, and physical abuse against Black girls and women continues to this day because for every Black woman who reports rape, at least 15 Black women refuse to report and one in four Black girls will be sexually abused before the age of 18 (Barlow, 2020; The National Center on Violence Against Women in the Black Community, 2018).

Even in our deaths, America forces Black girls and women to champion for recognition. As the pandemic continued, Black Americans witnessed the brutal murders of George Floyd and Ahmaud Arbery, and after weeks of protests, in both cases, their murderers were arrested. Yet, at the time this chapter was written, it has been five months and three days since Breonna Taylor was viciously murdered by police officers in her own home. Breonna's murder on March 13, 2020, occurred two months before the murders of George Floyd, and at the time of this writing, her murderers were still at-large. To honor her life, Breonna Taylor has now been beautifully portrayed on the cover of Vanity Fair, a fitting tribute, and a perfect example of interest convergence (Bell, 1980) at its finest. When discussing the tenet of interest convergence, Bell contends Brown vs. Board of Education was not attained because of America's beliefs of "liberty and justice for all." Instead, it was achieved because America needed to curtail the protests and demonstrations growing throughout the nation, push forward its Cold War Objectives, and promote desegregation as each of the three objectives limited economic expansion and capitalistic growth. Bell (1980) further argued that racial equality will only be achieved when it benefits the white interest. In short, Black liberation can only come when accompanying white comfort and when it secures white capitalistic gains.

This is particularly true when analyzing America's response to Breonna Taylor's murder. Albeit touching, the tributes by *Vanity Fair* and *Hulu* do not absolve Kentucky officers for Taylor's death. Suzanne Wolohan (2020) perfectly captured the frustration of many Black Americans when she stated:

> They used Breonna Taylor's image to sell *Vanity Fair*, now the *NY Times*. produced a Hulu movie about her. America will do anything except punish those cops. Always poised at the door, flowers in hand, waiting with breathless condolences. Reverence is not a substitute for justice.

Nor, I might add, is it a substitute for real love.

Taylor's death, like the deaths of many Black women, does not spark the same level of outrage. This lack of reciprocal love and awareness resulted in 2014, the creation of the #SayHerName Campaign by the African American Policy Forum (AAPF) and the Center for Intersectionality and Social Policy Studies (2015) who work to "illuminate police violence against Black women, we need to know who they are, how they lived, and why they suffered at the hands of police." To be clear, the Black Lives Matter Movement which has championed against police brutality of Black People in America, was founded by queer Black women. As Black girls and women's lives were repeatedly placed in danger, Black women once again took up the mantle, to create the #SayHerName campaign so that Black women and girls impacted by police violence would not be forgotten. As the movement demands, in this chapter focused on love, I say their names because as the Akan Peoples in Africa believe, if a name is uttered, a spirit will live (Akesson, 1965). I proudly say their names to praise their lives and mourn their loss to demonstrate the kind of thick love on which this book is based. It is a love inclusive of All Black Women – transgender, cisgender, and gender-nonconforming – because if one of us is unprotected, then we all are unprotected. It is a love that also includes names of Black girls and women who survived encounters with police officers, because death comes in many forms, and they all carry a burden of grief. I say their names to honor resilience and to engage in a communal healing love. I separate each name with a period as an explicit demand to love and protect the lives of Black girls and women. Periodt. #SayHerName.

Ma'Khia Bryant. Breonna Taylor. Atatiana Jefferson. Alexia Christian. Mya Hall. Miriam Carey. Gabrielle Nevarez. Shantel Davis. Malissa Williams. Sharmel Edwards. LaTonya Haggerty. Kendra James. Sandra Bland. Shelley Frey. Margaret Laverne Mitchell. Eleanor Bumpurs. Kathryn Johnston. Danette Daniels. Frankie Ann Perkins. Alberta Spruill. Tanisha Anderson. Michelle Cussesaux. Pearlie Golden. Shereese Francis. Kayla Moore. Tyisha Miller. Korryn Gaines. Natasha McKenna. Kyam Livingston. Sheneque Proctor. Rekia Boyd. Aiyana Stanley-Jones. Tarika Wilson. Megan Hockaday. Janisha Fonville. Aura Rosser. Yvette Smith. Duanna Johnson. Nizah Morris. New Jersey 7. Denise Stewart. Alesia Thomas. Rosann Miller. Sonji Taylor. Patricia Hartley (African American Policy Forum & Center for Intersectionality and Social Policy Studies, 2015; Cooper, 2020).

Many educators would believe that schools provide a safe and loving space for Black girls. Yet, as Derrick Bell proclaimed in *The Chronicle of the Sacrificed Black Child* (2005), the same racial violence occurring on America's streets occurs within America's classrooms. Black girls' bodies, hair, clothing, tones are policed, and their intelligence and integrity are questioned (Evans-Winters, 2019; Love, 2020; Morris, 2019). This is not thick love. Thrown into chaos, Black girls find themselves caught between respectability and assimilations politics, as if either will save them. Coined by Evelyn Rooks Higginbotham (1993) in her study of Black women in Church spaces, respectability politics utilize respectability narratives, or the belief that a person's morals, languages, looks, and sexualities should be like a dominant group, in this case, whiteness, as the basis for enacting social, political, and legal change. Respectability, in this manner, becomes an obstruction to prohibit Black expression, imagination, and existence. To be explicitly clear, sanctuary cannot be found in respectability. It did not save a teenage Black girl from being body-slammed in a Spring Valley High Classroom in Columbia, S. C (Associated Press, 2016). It did not protect two Black girls in Boston from being suspended for wearing Box Braids (Lazar, 2017). Respectability did not protect four 12-year-old girls in New York from being strip-searched because they were incredibly happy in the cafeteria (Ortiz, 2019a). In truth, respectability does not protect Black girls' childhoods from being interrupted, the adultification and objectification of their bodies, or the erasures which occur within classroom curriculums (Cooper, Morris, & Boylorn, 2017; Ife, 2017; Morris, 2016; Tolliver, 2018, 2020). These violent acts only prohibit Black girl magic and Black girl actualization from occurring. As Kellner and Share (2005) emphasize, "Coming to voice is important for people who have seldom been allowed to speak for themselves, but without critical analysis it is not enough" (p. 371). Again, I must reemphasize: Schools were never designed for Black bodies, the Black imagination, or Black resistance and resilience. For Black girls and the community of young Black women as a whole, it is imperative to have a space and an opportunity to give voice to their life experiences (Hill, 2016; Nyachae & Ohito, 2019; Tolliver, 2020).

This battle for Black girls and women to be recognized, affirmed, and protected does not just occur in America's public schools. In the halls of Academia – institutions of higher education – Black women are just as threatened and oppressed. African American Studies and anthropology scholar Christen A. Smith (2017) created the "Cite Black Women Movement" "to push people to engage in a radical praxis of citation that acknowledges and honors Black women's transnational intellectual production" (Smith, 2017). The movement advocates for five guiding principles for Black Women Scholars but connects as well to Black girls in schools. Smith asks for an emphasis on (1) reading Black women's work; (2) integrating Black women into the CORE academic syllabi; (3) acknowledging Black women's intellectual production; (4) making space for Black women to speak, and (5) giving Black women the space and time to breathe (Smith, 2017). The last principle, a demand for "time and space to breathe" illustrates the tenuous and stressful position America creates for Black girls and women: needing time and space to breathe while protecting others and simultaneously, needing time and space to breathe while saving ourselves. By failing to see Black girls and women in the totality of their humanity, American has only extolled fake love. Whether we are at homes in bed, walking the hallways of Academia or middle schools, or even leading the movements to save our very own lives, Black girls and women are always in need of sanctuary.

I tenaciously begin this chapter by providing illustrations of America's fake love. I do so because fake love or thin love is so prevalent that it is often used as a barometer of America's progress. For example, the persistence of a post-racial America and the absurd notion that because America had a Black president, we have somehow magically erased four centuries of Anti-Blackness. I have endured many discussions during equity and anti-racist professional development when educators have audaciously stated, "Enslavement has ended. The Civil Rights Movement has ended." These statements are not factual. Enslavement has not ended; it has just transformed in a profitable prison system and human trafficking network. The fight for civil rights continues to this day as the dream of equity, which was at the heart of the movement, was never achieved. In truth, it is the perennial quest for equity that has inspired the Black Lives Matter, Say Her Name, Flint Water Crisis, Me Too, and other racial justice movements. To demand my silence or complicity in my dehumanization is not justice, and it is most certainly not loving. Thick love, real love, as Zora Neale Hurston described, "makes your soul crawl out from its hiding place." Love demands that we face the inconsistent, messy, disparities that mark America's complex history. Love demands that we are fully transparent in acknowledging that America created a contentious space for Black people; a "there" Kinloch (2018) describes as

> A painful, destructive, hateful, and harm-ridden. It's both a place and a time, undefined by boundaries and exceeding any limitation. "There," unfortunately, is also a discourse and a system, heavily imbued with patriarchal, white supremacist, hetero-normative dispositions, behaviors, and economies that seek and often result in the perpetual oppression and, hence, the violent deaths of Black people. Without question, this type of "there" is difficult and dangerous, devastating, and deadly, particularly for Black people. And, yet it is this "there" that requires us to stand in solidarity, walk with purpose, and rely on revolutionary, humanizing, critical, and community-centric methods by which to seek and sustain our freedom.
>
> (p. 100)

"There" is the messy place where our work as transformational warriors begins. "There" moves beyond the performative allyship which only requires a brief donation of time. "There" requires that we sacrifice our privileges, which we did nothing to earn, and place ourselves in a position of danger to secure justice for someone else (Love, 2020). "There" requires we stand at the crosswalk of fear, courage, vulnerability, and raw truths. "There" is more than equity work or working for social justice. "There" is a spiritual commune where we, as Alice Walker proclaims, use our bodies, our intellects, our hearts, and our strengths in "activism as the rent for living on the planet" (Parmar, 2013).

Learning through Eyes of Thick Love: A Radical Love, Real Love

The first half of this chapter focused on discussions of fake love in a white supremacist society. Now, I turn to the spaces from which I draw real or radical love as critical to the support educators might find in the wisdom of those who can guide us if we let them. I first learned about the power of radical love and truth in my Southern Baptist Church. My pastor stood at the pulpit and his deep baritone reverberated through my bones as he read 1 Corinthians 13: 4–8, 12:

Love is patient, love is kind. It does not envy, it does not boast, it is not proud. It does not dishonor others, it is not self-seeking, it is not easily angered, it keeps no record of wrongs. Love does not delight in evil but rejoices with the truth. It always protects, always trusts, always hopes, always perseveres.

(KJV)

The words left my pastor's mouth and my soul devoured them. In that moment, I began to engage in critical introspection which I now call "soul speak," a complex raw and honest dialogue grounded in agape love (Smith, in progress). I passionately believe "soul speak" is but one of the many ways to counter the spirit murders (Love, 2020) which routinely occur in public school classrooms as Black students' identities, histories, languages, and verve are systematically degraded, silenced, or ignored. Imagine how educational spaces (both public and higher education) would look and feel if educators were worried that our lessons, grounded in love and truth, spoke to our students' souls as much as they spoke to mastering content standards.

As I grew older and moved beyond the protections of my Black family into the world of the southeastern primarily white university, I fully internalized how religion as an institution is entrenched in white supremacy, but it did not deter my spiritual sojourn with love; I just realized I needed additional teachers to name what I experienced. Fortunately, my college studies guided me to Critical Race Theory (CRT) and Black Feminist/Womanist Thought (Figure 3.1). The combination of these two lenses allowed me to create an oppositional gaze; it allowed me to look at my body and experiences and the experiences of the Blue

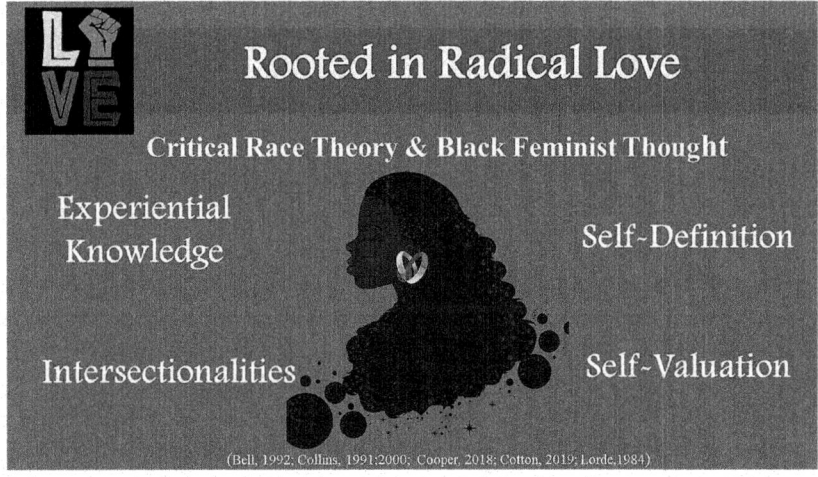

FIGURE 3.1 Theoretical Framework

Diamonds, my research partners, and love advocates, through eyes of love. Both theories tackle the complexities of race and racism associated with being Black and girl/woman in America. CRT examines the endemic nature of racism and the intersections of race and gender. It does not, however, directly address the Black girl/woman's bodies. The issue of the Black girlhood being both hypervisible while remaining partially invisible is dissected in Black Feminist Studies. Both theories help to problematize how obese Black girls/women view themselves through the distortion of the dominant ideology that lacks real love. June Jordan (1988) eloquently used the metaphor of the distorted mirror to illustrate this principle. She noted:

> We begin to group up in a house where every true mirror shows us the face of somebody who does not belong there, whose walk and whose talk will never look or sound 'right,' because that house was meant to shelter a family that is alien and hostile to us.
>
> (p. 161)

Critical Race Theory

CRT originated in legal scholarship with such pioneers as Derrick Bell (1992), Kimberlé Crenshaw (1991), Richard Delgado (2001), and Mari Matsuda (1993). Evolving from Critical Legal Studies (CLS), CRT challenged the fundamental failings of the court system to create and sustain meaningful reform (Ladson-Billings, 2009). Whereas CLS critiqued liberalism it did truly little to address the deeply rooted role of racism in American life (West, 1993). Legal scholars realized that new theories and strategies were necessary to challenge more subtle forms of racism (Delgado, Stefancic, & Harris, 2017). Loosely defined, CRT is

> a strategy that accounts for the role of race and racism in U.S. education and works toward the elimination of racism as part of a larger goal of eliminating other forms of subordination such as gender, class, and sexual orientation.
>
> (Yosso, Delgado-Bernal, & Solorzano, 1998, p. 90)

A traditional perspective of racism would contend racism is an extraordinary occurrence which is willingly enacted by individuals who are propelled by extreme hatred. In contrast, a critical view of racism argues racism is institutionalized and occurs on a daily basis; it is sanctioned through color-blind policies and discourse and is sustained by actions assumed to apply fairly to all (Bell, 1992; Delgado et al., 2017). Therefore, CRT analyzes how race, racism, and power maneuver with individuals, groups, or institutions in the American society by deconstructing dominant ideology and discourse, challenging hegemonic forces that marginalize and oppress people of Color, and providing a platform for social transformation by reconstructing agency and power distribution (Bell, 1992; Delgado et al., 2017; Ladson-Billings, 1998).

CRT is a set of interrelated beliefs comprised of five main tenets. It (a) acknowledges racism is endemic in American life and is observed and felt at various legal, cultural, and psychological levels (Tate, 1997); (b) challenges the dominant ideology of neutrality, objectivity, colorblindness, and meritocracy (Delgado et al., 2017); (c) challenges white supremacy as the notion of whiteness as property (Bell, 1992; Ladson-Billings, 1998); (d) recognizes the intersectionality and compounding jeopardies of race, racism, and power with other forms of oppression such as sexism or classism (Soloranzo & Yosso, 2001); (e) recognizes the power and legitimacy of experiential knowledge and voices of Color (Ladson-Billings, 1998; Soloranzo & Yosso, 2001). Four of these tenets are pertinent for this study: Racism's endemic presence, whiteness as property, intersectionalities, and experiential knowledge from voices of Color as transformative sites.

From a CRT perspective, racism cannot be rigidly defined by acts of overt discrimination or violence against people of Color; instead, racism must be understood as a more institutionalized and nuanced presence that is interwoven into the fabric of our lives and is often unrecognizable by those with power and privilege (Bell, 1992; Delgado et al., 2017; Ladson-Billings, 1998). The belief of racial realism is that racism is a permanent fixture. Critics would argue that we live in a post-racial America (Delgado et al., 2017) where the dreams and goals of the Civil Rights era have been achieved and that with hard work and dedication, anyone can make it. The myth of post-racial America is just as strong as the myth of meritocracy (Delgado et al., 2017) and does not give credence to the ongoing struggles of Blacks in America to make progress in a society which would deny its existence.

Since our forced appearance on America's shores, Blacks have held a precarious position. "Tolerated in good times, despised when things go wrong, as a people we [Blacks] are scapegoated and sacrificed as distraction or catalyst for compromise to facilitate resolution of political differences or relieve economic adversity" (Bell, 1992, p. 7). Nearly 22 years after Bell wrote these words, this fact still holds true. Being born Black in America means a daily struggle to remain visible and heard in a society which would deem you invisible and mute unless your presence can enhance society or individuals' vitality or livelihood. In truth, being Black in America means striving to uplift and redefine oneself in a society laden with racial disparities by health, education, employment, income, and wealth. The reasons given for these disparities regularly put the blame unjustly on those who suffer the consequences of these statistics rather than on the systems of oppression, privilege, profiling, and discrimination that lead to them. The statistics are unsettling:

- The typical Black household earns a fraction of white households – just 59 cents for every dollar. The gap between Black and white annual household incomes is about $29,000 per year.

- Black Americans are over twice as likely to live in poverty as white Americans.
- Black children are three times as likely to live in poverty as white children.
- The median wealth of Black families ($17,000) – is less than one-tenth that of white families ($171,000).
- The wealth gap between Black and white households increases with education.
- Much less than half (42%) of Black families own their homes, compared to almost three-quarters (73%) of white families.
- Persistent segregation leads to large disparities in the quality of secondary education, leading to worse economic outcomes.
- The incarceration rate for Black Americans is falling but is still nearly six times the rate for white Americans (Joint Economic Committee, 2020).

After analyzing the data, it is easy to understand that although race is not biologically real, it is socially and politically constructed via law, public policy, and social practice to perpetuate power structures historically designed to create race so that dominance is assured (Coates, Ferber, & Brunsma, 2018). The effects of this design are far-reaching and pervasive across generations (Matthew, 2018). From society, we are flooded by the message, "race is only skin deep." Culp (1998) countered this belief by stating, "race is only skin deep, but white supremacy runs to the core … and the work of Critical Race Theory is to go beyond the socially constructed boundaries understanding race's importance" (p. 1639).

Finally, Ladson-Billings (1998) emphasized Delgado's (1989) rationale for understanding the importance of experiential knowledge and voices of Color by stating, "it provides members of the out-group a vehicle for psychic self-preservation and the exchange of stories from teller to listener can help overcome ethnocentrism and the dysconscious (cited in King, 1991) drive or need to view the world in one way" (Ladson-Billings, 1998, p. 23). In a discourse and construct where fat or obese bodies are read as lazy, gluttonous, or lacking moral fortitude (Cox, 2020; Oliver, 2006; Taylor, 2018), experiential knowledge provides a site for a counterstory and reconstruction of mainstream ideology. In this manner, CRT challenges the many distortions, omissions, and deficit thinking embedded in traditional school curriculum and creates a space for critical analysis.

Black Feminist/Womanist Studies

Black Feminist Studies was an outcome of the Civil Rights struggles and the feminist movement of the 1960s and 1970s. Pioneered by such greats as Frances Beale (Beale, 1971), Patricia Hill Collins (1991), Audre Lorde (1984), bell hooks (1981), and Angela Davis (1983), Black Feminist Studies argues that Black women are positioned differently in oppressive power structures than their white girl or Black boy counterparts. Unlike traditional feminist critique, which is largely grounded in the white girlhood experience, Black Feminist Studies "probes the silences, erasures, distortions, and complexities surrounding the experiences of African-American women" (Guy-Sheftall, 2009, p. 11). Kimberlé Crenshaw (1989) described how Black women were often excluded from feminist studies because it was "predicated on a discrete set of experiences that often did not accurately reflect the interaction of race and gender" (p. 58). Therefore, Black Feminist Studies is grounded in the principle of intersectionality which postulates that oppressive patterns are interrelated and influenced by intersecting systems including race, gender, class, ability, ethnicity, and size (Collins, 2015). These converging identities create compounding jeopardies which cannot be fully explained by examining each identity in isolation.

In *Black Looks: Race and Representation*, hooks (1992) examined the intricacies of analyzing the Black girls' shape by discussing how media and its representation of the Black girls' form are used as pedagogical tools which oppress and exploit. Using this lens, the body may be viewed as a text which can be read and a text to which society can add meaning. hooks argues while promoting the hegemony of the thin white ideal, Black women and adolescent girls are marginalized and their beauty is not seen as being worthy of visibility and desire. These ideals become prototypes which African American women and girls use to assess and judge their bodies (Melancon & Braxton, 2015).

Black feminist theorist Collins (2000) claimed this homogenized approach to beauty removes racial and ethnic differences that disturb the thin white norm. Thinness becomes a dominant ideology to which all must subscribe. This is done through the bombardment of media, film, music, and social media which all reinforce white supremacy with the goal being the annihilation of Black girl/women subjectivities (hooks, 1992, 2005). According to Black feminists, beauty, then, is not a matter of objectivity; it is a matter of judgment. Theorists have long contended social values can be read through the body (Bordo, 1993; Cahnman, 1968; Cameron & Russell, 2016) In Eurocentric society, the thin white frame denotes happiness, success, and social acceptability (Melancon & Braxton, 2015). In contrast, the obese Black frame is perceived as being deviant, lazy, or excessive (Oliver, 2006; Taylor, 2018). Framing the Black girls' bodies in this manner is oppressive and creates a whirlwind of emotion including self-loathing, guilt, and rage (Cox, 2020; Taylor, 2018). Furthermore, since many Black girls have not critically confronted these images, they have no way to acknowledge, name, and speak their pain (Collins, 2016; hooks, 1989, 1992, 2005) and thereby prohibiting healing.

This suffering and marginalization of women of Color as they internalize negative representations has been a corner of Black Feminist Thought (Beal, 1979; Davis, 1983; Lorde, 1984). To resist racist representations Black girls must confront the colonizing ideology by developing a critical consciousness (Collins, 2016; hooks, 1990b). This requires Black girls to critique representations for falsehoods and create new forms of representations which uplift the Black body. hooks argued (1992)

> As long as black folks are taught that the only way we can … be materially privileged is by first rejecting blackness, our history and culture, and then there will always be a crisis in black identity. Internalized racism will continue to erode collective struggle for self-determination.
>
> (p. 18)

In short, we must confront massive hate by fully loving and embracing our Blackness. Participation in this study allowed five Black adolescent girls to build a critical conscious in a space designed to allow them to voice their emotional and psychological turmoil.

Being members of a critical and collaborative community which centered dialogues on race, gender, size, and the myriad of intersectionalities which exist within and across those dialogues, allowed the participants in this study to "engage in critical dialogue without fear of emotional collapse" in spaces where they could "hear and know one another in difference and complexities of experience" (hooks, 1994b, p. 110). When such transformation takes place, schools and teachers create places of sanctuary against white domination and hegemonic forces. By invoking Black Feminism, Black adolescent girls can view the world through a dual lens which creates an awakened consciousness and an empowered individual; both states are vital for social, political, and educational reform.

Guiding Wisdoms, Dual Lens: Intersectionalities and Experiential Knowledge

If the theory is the proverbial camera, an instrument which affords the opportunity to take snapshots of the world to make predictions, analyze patterns, or note discrepancies according to a particular paradigm, research base, and/or ideology, then applying both CRT and Black Feminist Theory to the camera only sharpens and refines the image. The combination of the dual lenses allows both the researcher and reader to use CRT to closely analyze and interrogate the presence and use of racial realism and whiteness as a property while drawing on Black Feminist theory to understand how self-definition and self-valuation can be used as resistance strategies. Dual lenses also allow the investigation of connections within and across the tenets of the two complementing theories: intersectionalities and experiential knowledge until a picture which was once distorted comes into a heightened sense of focus and awareness.

When reflecting on the importance of stories told about her and those she tells about others, Chimamanda Adichie (2010) explained, "The single story creates stereotypes, and the problem with stereotypes is not that they are untrue, but that they are incomplete. They make one story become the only story."

Adichie is resoundingly accurate because she recognizes that many lenses shape our experiences and tint our view of the world; for this study, those lenses incorporate perceptions of gender, race, and body size. In much the same way, a theoretical framework grounds how researchers recognize, name, evaluate, and write about the spaces, places, people, and events in their work. Thus, theory selection must be an introspective and reflective process. Both CRT and Black Feminist Theory were carefully chosen because they celebrate the strength of intersectional identities and experiential knowledge. These overlapping identities provide knowledge and wisdom which must be shared in an innovative and liberatory format. For this reason, I assert this entire book as an example of ethnopoetics. This powerful theoretical combination and liberating format allow for new stories, often the stories overlooked because they are deemed unworthy, to be shared with the world. By doing so, these two theories provide a counternarrative to fake love, by demonstrating the possibility of an affirming and radical love.

Jahraymecofasola: A New Way to Love Blackness

To discuss the complexities of Black love, I must invoke King's (2005) Dimensions of Black Culture as the concept of love cannot be expressed in words alone: it must be felt through spirituality, movement, rhythm, and harmony. It must be expressed through adaptions, verve, affect, improvisation, and social-time perspectives. As it flows from the Black body, Black love needs a myriad of ways to manifest itself. When the words themselves fall short, we create new ones: a Jahraymecofasola love (Jill Scott, 2015), a new word in a mother tongue, that expresses a love that "makes me who I are." A love so real, and potent, it must be said in my heart speak, Black English to demonstrate that this love is so powerful, it resonates through time and affirms our past, present, and future selves. Moore (2018) contends:

> Love, true love, Black radical love is a practice—a ritual, one must take up daily. It is a practice of protecting Black life and emptying ourselves of the death-dealing practices of misogyny; trans and queer antagonism; ableism; elitism; ageism; and any other act of lovelessness that aids in the killing of Black people's spirits/bodies. This love ... is central to the current iteration of the Black struggle for liberation.
>
> (p. 326)

Love in this manner is more than a noun; it is a verb, an intentional action that must be purposefully chosen (hooks, 2000; Moore, 2018; Ohito, 2018). This radical love is rooted in Blackness and is a fusion of "care, affection, recognition, respect, commitment, trust, as well as open and honest communication" (hooks, 2000, p. 40). This radical love is racialized and affective (Ohito, 2018) and induces its practitioners to note how "transcending the self and produces new forms of political communities" (Nash, 2011, p. 3).

This need to transcend the self is key to analyzing the fake love permeating education as an institution. Transcending self means a willingness to move past ego, privileges, and self-interest to become servants of truth. I've often heard colleagues in schools proclaim, "I love all of my students." At first, hearing the statement sounds loving, but it requires a more critical analysis. One that can only come by asking how can you love? How can you love when your classroom pedagogy and curriculum centers whiteness and Eurocentric ideals? How can you love your students when they never read stories of triumph from a rich Black literary heritage? How can you love your students when you know cursory information about their families and communities? How can you love your students when you do not see them past a data point? How can you love your students if you do not see color? One cannot love by denying a people's stories, realities, and experiences. Johnson, Stovall, & Baszile (2017) argue, if we are about the work of radical love and transformation:

> ELA teachers and literacy educators must start 'loving Blackness to death.' In Black English, we say we "love something or someone to death" or as some Black adults say, we "love the hell out of something or someone"— to love someone to death and to love the hell out of someone is to have strong feelings and admiration for someone that one will love her or him unconditionally until one no longer exists in physical form and beyond physical death.
>
> (p. 63)

This love knows no boundaries and eclipses self, time, and space. It is this revolutionary love which is needed in classrooms.

To advise how to love Blackness to death, I stood on the shoulders of Black literary giants as their words have longed been a truth space and refuge for me. I offer these insights in Table 3.1.

Through Walker's (1989) *The Gospel According to Shug*, I learned that love and service are deeply intertwined. Service means seeing beyond myself, "my family, my country "and my goals for the good of the greater community. Being of service means a commitment to loving and protecting the Black body. Many white educators who refuse to advocate and participate in movements such as #Sayhername and #BLM believe their silence and inaction does not inflict harm upon them. Menakem (2017) debunks this myth by stating how we must reimagine the body as site of trauma and of liberation and reminds us "trauma and healing are not just private experiences. Sometimes trauma is a collective experience, in which case our approaches for mending must be collective and communal as well" (p. 13). Being a bystander to the symbolic and physical violence

TABLE 3.1 Reflections on Truth and Love

Truth Lesson	Love Alignment Lesson
(1) Multiple truths can exist side by side. (2) All truths, like all stories, are legitimate and valuable. (3) There are multiple ways of expressing our truths.	"HELPED are those who love the entire cosmos rather than their own tiny country, city, or farm, for to them will be shown the unbroken web of life and the meaning of infinity…HELPED are those who risk themselves for others' sakes; to them will be given increasing opportunities for ever greater risks. Theirs will be a vision of the world in which no one's gift is despised or lost" (Walker, 1989, pp. 287–288). "Then you must tell 'em dat love ain't somethin' lak uh grindstone dat's de same thing everywhere and do de same thing tuh everything it touch. Love is lak de sea. It's uh movin' thing, but still and all, it takes its shape from de shore it meets, and it's different with every shore" (Hurston, 1937, p. 128)
(4) Denying, negating, or ignoring truths is a traumatic and violent act. (5) Sharing our truths, like telling our stories, is a harbinger of healing and liberation. (6) Truth-telling, much like love, is rooted in justice. There can be no justice without truth.	"The moment we choose to love we begin to move against domination, against oppression. The moment we choose to love we begin to move towards freedom, to act in ways that liberate ourselves and others. That action is the testimony of love as the practice of freedom" (hooks, 1994a, p. 298). "Love takes off masks that we fear we cannot live without and know we cannot live within. I use the word 'love' here not merely in the personal sense but as a state of being, or a state of grace — not in the infantile American sense of being made happy but in the tough and universal sense of quest and daring and growth" (Baldwin, 1963, p. 95).

impacting Black lives, not only in America but also globally, traumatizes the psyche. Transformation requires a collective action and will nurture collective healing.

Hurston's *Their Eyes Were Watching God* (1937) reminds us that love evolves. Although written in 1937, we must further contextualize this quote in the time of #BLM in the wake of the death of Breonna Taylor. Hardison and Jelks (2017) maintain, "love still matters in our communities – whether it is hot romantic love, queer love, family love, or self-love. *Their Eyes Were Watching God* reminds us that we must think about the ethics of our love, too" (para. 6). Love does not collapse upon itself; it expands and becomes inclusive of those who are needing love. Then authentically love Blackness … we love Blackness in its myriad of forms. With this critical lens, love becomes a political, restorative, and spiritual tool for change.

hooks' *All About Love* (2000) speaks to love's liberating power and the courage needed to reside and work in love. It takes courage to face a system of oppression and dismantle it and requires mindsets shifts for both the marginalized and majority groups. We have all mis-educated (Woodson, 1933) and must all do the work to unlearn the lies they told us (Loewen, 2018). Monahan (2011) states:

> For those who are members of exploited or oppressed groups, this means taking up the project of mental decolonization—of confronting internalized racism and sexism, self-hatred, guilt, and despair. For those who are members of dominant groups, this means turning an unblinking eye toward our own beliefs and practices so that we can recognize and acknowledge when we have failed to live up to the ideals we espouse. Since many people can occupy both of these positions at once, or in different ways at different times and places, part of this education for critical consciousness can involve learning to understand our roles—as both dominator and dominated throughout the course of our lives.
>
> (pp. 107–108)

A critical consciousness is vital in utilizing a critical introspection to note, acknowledge, and remedy our biases, privileges, and prejudices. Critical consciousness also takes a commitment to communal love. "Communal love runs deep and is grounded in the affirmation that your existence, your successes, your pain and your wounds are all welcomed as legitimate cultural capital and profound spaces of knowing" (Smith, 2018, p. 116).

James Baldwin's *The Fire Next Time* (1963) is a profound love letter to America in which he analyzes love's nuanced complexities. Baldwin expounds on the notion that love is growth. Love cannot exist in stagnation. It forces us to confront our real selves – the ones who lay hidden behind masks of status, respectability, inaction, willful ignorance, and silence. Love is not a destination at which we haphazardly arrive. Instead, love is drenched in the possibility of becoming the next iteration of our best selves. Just as love evolves, so should we.

The wisdom of those who write about radical love in these ways allows me to walk in love in times when I am least hopeful about the world's destruction of Blackness. I walk in love with my Islamic, Hinduist, Buddhist, Indigenous, Sikhist, Jewish, Atheistic believers and I walk with individuals who seek to understand the Devine in many other ways and those who do not. For me, the notion of radical love takes me back to the text which served as my primer on love, words that no critical theorist has been able to enhance:

> Love is patient, love is kind. It does not envy, it does not boast, it is not proud.[5] It does not dishonor others, it is not self-seeking, it is not easily angered, it keeps no record of wrongs.[6] Love does not delight in evil but rejoices with the truth.[7] It always protects, always trusts, always hopes, always perseveres.

I ask you now to pause and reflect upon your personal and professional choices. I ask you to stare deeply into the depths of your soul and contemplate the following:

- Are we demonstrating teaching with a love ethic when we lose patience and angrily scream at our students?
- Are we demonstrating teaching with a love ethic when we discuss a student's behavioral record with colleagues?
- Are we demonstrating teaching with a love ethic when we detail a student's mistakes individually or publicly?
- Are we demonstrating teaching with a love ethic when we utilize a curriculum which diminishes the achievements of people?
- Are we demonstrating teaching with a love ethic when we display a revisionist history which minimizes the atrocities and contradictory behavior of historical/contemporary figures?
- Are we demonstrating a love ethic when we fail to learn more about our students' many situated identities?
- Are we demonstrating a love ethic when we focus on how much money we spend in our classes instead of how those contributions are leveling an unequal playing field?
- Are we demonstrating a love ethic when we deny our students' languages and histories?
- Are we demonstrating a love ethic when we fail to persevere to learn more students' families and their communities?
- Are we demonstrating a love ethic when we purposefully refuse to make learning about marginalized populations a topic for continuous professional development and growth?
- Are we demonstrating a love ethic when we fail to see the myriad of possibilities that lay in each child?

These questions are not meant to promote guilt and shame. Those emotions root us in stagnation, and as previously stated, love cannot foster there. Instead, these questions are meant to begin the process of critical introspection to transform our ideals into beliefs for a new educational system which loves, values, and centers Black lives. This is not about guilt. Instead, these questions serve as a call to action, because now that you know better, you must do better. Let us grow and walk in love.

Loving Black Girls Means Loving Black Bodies

Though the Black obese body will never meet white mainstream society's mark of desirability because of racism's endemic presence (Bell, 1992) it is still expected to strive to obtain this lofty objective. Ironically, it is these failed attempts at desirability which serve to further mar the spirit and nurture further confusion (Cox, 2020; Jones & Shorter-Goodman, 2003; Taylor, 2018). Obese Black girls/women's form is confined to a "house" that never has or, accepting the tenant of racial realism, never will love its inherent beauty. Existing within such warring ideals, trying to love the obese body while being simultaneously told to abhor it, prohibits liberation and reifies the thin white ideal (Cox, 2020; hooks, 1992).

Traditionally, the stories of Black girls have been misrepresented, overlooked, or completely unwritten; however, the significance of these experiences can no longer be cast aside (Evans-Winters, 2019; Morris, 2019). We must endeavor to analyze those same experiences so that we may learn more and better prepare and inform the next generations. Amir, Marie, Jennifer, Kelsey, and Melody provide an insight into the deliberate pedagogical moves necessary to provide sanctuary for Black girls in education. Dotson (2013) declares educators must: (1) make a commitment to Black girls and their literacies and (2) trust the knowledges which are inherent in Black girls. By doing so, love becomes inseparable from belief (3) and understand daring to love means committing to dismantling oppressive institutions. These moves are the foundation of creating a sanctuary that is a truth space. It is through these communal experiences and knowledges found within that sanctuary that we gain insight into the political, social, economic, and cultural impetus that accompanies being Black and being a girl.

References

Adichie, C. (2010, June). *The danger of a single story [Video blog post]*. https://www.ted.com/talks/chimamanda_adichie_the_danger_of_a_single_story?language=en

African American Policy Forum (AAPF), & Center for Intersectionality and Social Policy Studies. (2015). *Say her name: Resisting police brutality against black women* (pp. 1–45, Rep.). African American Policy Forum & Center for Intersectionality and Social Policy Studies.

Akesson, A. (1965). The Akan concept of the soul. *African Affairs, 64* (257), 280–291.

Associated Press. (2016, September). *Deputy who tossed a S.C. High school student won't be charged* (Published 2016). https://www.nytimes.com/2016/09/03/afternoonupdate/deputy-who-tossed-a-sc-high-school-student-wont-be-charged.html

Baldwin, J. (1963). *Fire next time*. Dial Press.

Barlow, J. (2020, February 20). *Black women: The forgotten survivors of sexual assault*. https://www.apa.org/pi/about/newsletter/2020/02/black-women-sexual-assault

Beale, F. (1971). *Double jeopardy: To be Black and female*. Radical Education Project.

Bell, D. (1992). *Faces at the bottom of the well: The permanence of racism*. Basic Books.

Bell, D., Delgado, R., & Stefancic, J. (2005). *The Derrick Bell reader*. New York University Press.

Bell, D. A. (1980). Brown v. Board of education and the interest-convergence dilemma. *Harvard Law Review, 93*(3), 518–533. doi:10.2307/1340546

Benia, C. O. (2018). *Medical bondage: Race, gender, and the origins of American gynecology*. The University of Georgia Press.

Bordo, S. (1993). *Unbearable weight: Feminism, Western culture, and the body*. University of California Press.

Cahnman, W. (1968). The stigma of obesity. *The Sociological Quarterly*, *93*(3), 283–299.
Cameron, E., & Russell, C. (2016). *The fat pedagogy reader: Challenging weight-based oppression through critical education (counterpoints)* (New ed.). Peter Lang Inc., International Academic Publishers.
Coates, R. D., Ferber, A. L., & Brunsma, D. L. (2018). *The matrix of race: Social construction, intersectionality, and inequality*. SAGE Publications.
Collins, P. H. (1991). *Black feminist thought: Knowledge, consciousness, and the politics of empowerment*. Routledge.
Collins, P. H. (2015). No guarantees: Symposium on Black feminist thought. *Ethnic and Racial Studies*, *38* (13), 2349–2354. doi:10.1080/01419870.2015.1058512
Collins, P. H. (2016). Black feminist thought as oppositional knowledge. *Departures in Critical Qualitative Research*, 5(3), 133–144. doi:10.1525/dcqr.2016.5.3.133.
Cooper, B. (2020, June 04). *Why are Black women and girls still an afterthought?* https://time.com/5847970/police-brutality-black-women-girls/
Cooper, B. C., Morris, S. M., & Boylorn, R. M. (2017). *The crunk feminist collection*. Feminist Press at the City University of New York.
Cox, J. (2020). *Fat girls in black bodies: Creating communities of our own*. North Atlantic Books.
Crenshaw, K. (1989). Demarginalizing the intersection of race and sex: A black feminist critique of antidiscrimination doctrine, feminist theory and antiracist politics. *The University of Chicago Legal Forum*, 139–167.
Crenshaw, K. (1991). Mapping the margins: Intersectionality, identity politics, and violence against women of color. *Stanford Law Review*, *43*(6), 1241–1299.
Culp, J. (1998). To the bone: Race and White privilege. *Minnesota Law Review*, *83*, 1637–1679.
Davis, A. Y. (1983). *Women, race, and class*. Vintage Books.
DeGruy, J. (2005). *Post traumatic slave syndrome: Americas legacy of enduring injury and healing*, revised ed. Upton Press.
Delgado, R. (1989). Storytelling for oppositionists and others: A plea for narrative. *Michigan Law Review*, *87*(8), 2411.
Delgado, R., & Stefancic, J. (2001). *Critical race theory: An introduction*. New York University Press.
Delgado, R., Stefancic, J., & Harris, A. P. (2017). *Critical race theory: An introduction*. New York University Press.
Dotson, K. (2013). Radical love. *The Black Scholar*, *43*(4), 38–45. doi:10.1080/00064246.2013.11413663
Evans-Winters, V. E. (2011). *Teaching Black girls: Resiliency in urban classrooms*. P. Lang.
Evans-Winters, V. E. (2019). *Black feminism in qualitative inquiry: A mosaic for writing our daughter's body*. Routledge.
Guy-Sheftall, B. (2009). Black feminist studies: The case of Anna Julia Cooper. *African American Review*, *43*(1), 11–15.
Hardison, A., & Jelks, R. (2017, March 21). *Zora Neale Hurston's radical Black love*. https://www.aaihs.org/zora-neale-hurstons-radical-black-love/
Higginbotham, E. R. (1993). *Righteous discontent: The women's movement in the Black Baptist Church, 1880–1920*. Harvard University Press.
Hill, D. C. (2016). Blackgirl, one word: Necessary transgressions in the name of imagining Black girlhood. *Cultural Studies ↔ Critical Methodologies*, *19*(4), 275–283. doi:10.1177/1532708616674994
hooks, B. (1989). *Talking back: Thinking feminist, thinking black*. South End Press.

hooks, B. (1990a). *Yearning: Race, gender, and cultural politics*. South End Press.
hooks, B. (1990b). Marginality as site of resistance. In R. Ferguson, T. T. Minh-Ha, & C. West (Eds.), *Out there: Marginalization and contemporary cultures*(pp. 341–343). The New Museum of Contemporary Art.
hooks, B. (1992). *Black looks: Race and representation*. South End Press.
hooks, B. (1994a). *Outlaw culture: Resisting representation*. Routledge, Taylor & Francis Group.
hooks, B. (1994b). *Teaching to transgress: Education as the practice of freedom*. Routledge.
hooks, B. (2000). *All about love: New visions*. William Morrow
hooks, B. (2005). *Sisters of the yam Black women and self-recovery*. South End Press.
Hurston, Z. N. (1937). *Their eyes were watching God*. J. B. Lippincott.
Ife, F. (2017). *Perhaps a Black girl rolls her eyes because it's one way she attempts to shift calcified pain throughout her body.* https://educate.bankstreet.edu/occasional-paper-series/vol2017/iss38/4
Jacobs, M. (2017). The violent state: Black women's invisible struggle against police violence. *UF Law Scholarship Repository, 24* (39), 39–100.
Johnson, L. L., Boutte, G., Greene, G., & Smith, D. E. (2018). *African diaspora literacy: The heart of transformation in K-12 schools and teacher education*. Lexington Books.
Johnson, L. L., Stovall, D. T., & Brazile, D. (2017). "Loving Blackness to death": (Re)imagining ELA classrooms in a time of racial chaos. *English Journal, 106*(4), 60–66.
Joint Economic Committee (JEC). (2020). The Economic State of Black America in 2020. Retrieved July 2020, from The Economic State of Black America in 2020.
Jones, C., & Shorter-Gooden, K. (2003). *Shifting: The double lives of Black women in America*. HarperCollins.
Jordan, J. (1988). Nobody mean more to me than you and the future life of Willie Jordan. *Harvard Educational Review, 58*(3), 363–375
Kellner, D., & Share, J. (2005). Toward critical media literacy: Core concepts, debates, organizations, and policy. *Discourse: Studies in the Cultural Politics of Education, 26*(3), 369–386.
King, J. E. (1991). Dysconscious racism: Ideology, identity, and the miseducation of teachers. *The Journal of Negro Education, 60*(2), 133–146.
King, J. E. (2005). *Black education: A transformative research and action agenda for the new century*. L. Erlbaum.
Kinloch, V. (2018). Commitment and danger, black life and black love: Toward radical possibilities. *Taboo: The Journal of Culture and Education, 17*(1), 69–78. doi:10.31390/taboo.17.1.08
Ladson-Billings, G. (1998). Just what is critical race theory and what's it doing in a nice field like education? *International Journal of Qualitative Studies in Education, 11*(1), 7–24.
Ladson-Billings, G. (2009). Just what is critical race theory and what's it doing in a nice field like education? In E. Taylor & D. Gillborn (Eds.), *Foundations of critical race theory in education* (pp. 17–36). Routledge.
Lazar, K. (2017, May 12). Black Malden charter students punished for braided hair extensions. *The Boston Globe*. https://www.bostonglobe.com/metro/2017/05/11/black-students-malden-school-who-wear-braids-face-punishment-parents-say/stWDlBSCJhw1zocUWR1QMP/story.html
Loewen, J. W. (2018). *Lies my teacher told me for young readers: Everything your American history textbook got wrong*. The New Press.
Lorde, A. (1984). *Sister outsider: Essays and speeches*. Crossing Press.

Love, B. (2020). *We want to do more than survive: Abolitionist teaching and the pursuit of educational freedom*. Beacon Press.

Matsuda, M. J. (1993). *Words that wound: Critical race theory, assaultive speech, and the First Amendment*. Westview Press.

Matthew, D. B. (2018). *Just medicine: A cure for racial inequality in American health care*. New York University Press.

Melancon, T., & Braxton, J. M. (2015). *Black female sexualities*. Rutgers University Press.

Menakem, R. (2017). *My grandmother's hands: Racialized trauma and the pathway to mending our hearts and bodies*. Central Recovery Press.

Milner, H. R., & Laughter, J. C. (2014). But good intentions are not enough: Preparing teachers to center race and poverty. *The Urban Review, 47*(2), 341–363.

Monahan, M. J. (2011). On the emancipatory thought of bell hooks. *The CLR James Journal, 17*, 102–111. doi:10.5840/clrjames20111717

Moore, D. L. (2018). Black radical love: A practice. *Public Integrity, 20*(4), 325–328. doi:10.1080/10999922.2018.1439564

Morris, M. W. (2016). *Pushout: The criminalization of Black girls in schools*. New Press.

Morris, M. W. (2019). *Sing a rhythm, dance a blues: Education for the liberation of Black and Brown girls*. The New Press.

Morrison, T. (1987). *Beloved*. Alfred A. Knopf.

Nash, J. (2011). Practicing love: Black feminism, Love-politics, and post-intersectionality. *Meridians: Feminism, Race, Transnationalism, 11*(2), 1–24.

Nyachae, T. M., & Ohito, E. O. (2019). No disrespect: A womanist critique of respectability discourses in extracurricular programming for Black girls. *Urban Education*, 1–31. doi:10.1177/0042085919893733

Ohito, E. O. (2018). "I Just Love Black People!": Love, pleasure, and critical pedagogy in urban teacher education. *The Urban Review, 51*(1), 123–145.

Oliver, J. E. (2006). *Fat politics: The real story behind America's obesity epidemic*. Oxford University Press.

Ortiz, E. (2019a, December 21). *Fort Worth police officer who fatally shot Atatiana Jefferson indicted on murder charge*. https://www.nbcnews.com/news/us-news/fort-worth-police-officer-who-fatally-shot-atatiana-jefferson-indicted-n1105916

Ortiz, E. (2019b, April 30). *Four girls at N.Y. middle school subjected to 'dehumanizing' strip search, lawsuit says*. https://www.nbcnews.com/news/us-news/four-girls-n-y-middle-school-subjected-dehumanizing-strip-search-n1000321

Parmar, P. (Writer). (2013, July 8). Alice Walker: Beauty in truth [Television series episode]. In *Alice Walker: Beauty in Truth*. BBC.

Raines, H. P. (1983, July 24). *The Birmingham Bombing*. https://www.nytimes.com/1983/07/24/magazine/the-birmingham-bombing.html

Rosenfelt, D. (2019). In love and trouble: Stories of Black women. *Radical Teacher, 113*, 4–7. doi:10.5195/rt.2019.565

Smith, C. (2017). *Cite black women*. https://www.citeblackwomencollective.org/

Smith, D. E. (2016, December). Finding sanctuary in sisterhood: A middle school literacy group critically analyzes race, gender, and size [Doctoral dissertation]. University of South Carolina.

Smith, D. E. (2018). Telling our stories; sharing our lives: Storytelling as the heart of resistance. In L. L. Johnson, G. Boutte, G. Greene, & D. E. Smith (Eds.), *African diaspora literacy: The heart of transformation in K-12 schools and teacher education* (pp. 107–125). Lexington Books, an imprint of The Rowman & Littlefield Publishing Group.

Solorzano, D. G., & Yosso, T. J. (2001). Critical race and LatCrit theory and method: Counter-storytelling. *International Journal of Qualitative Studies in Education, 14*(4), 471–495. doi:10.1080/09518390110063365

Tate, W. F. (1997). Chapter 4: Critical race theory and education: History, theory, and implications. *Review of Research in Education, 22*(1), 195–247.

Taylor, S. R. (2018). *The body is not an apology: the power of radical self-love.* Barrett-Koehler.

The National Center on Violence Against Women in the Black Community. (2018). *Black Women and Sexual Assault* (pp. 1–2, Rep. No. 09EV0432). Ujima.

Tolliver, S. (2018). Alterity and innocence: The hunger games, rue, and black girl adultification. *Journal of Children's Literature, 44*(2), 4–15.

Tolliver, S. (2020). "We wouldn't have the same connection": Using read-alouds to build community with Black girls. *Voices from the Middle, 27*(4), 24–27.

Walker, A. (1989). *The temple of my familiar.* Harcourt.

West, C. (1993). *Race matters.* Beacon Press.

Winn, M. T. (2011). *Girl time: Literacy, justice, and the school-to-prison pipeline.* Teachers College Press.

Woodson, C. G. (1933). *The miseducation of the Negro.* Africa World Press.

Yosso, T., Delgado-Bernal, D., & Solorzano, D. (1998). Critical race theory, race and gender microaggressions, and the experience of Chicana and Chicano scholars. *International Journal of Qualitative Studies in Education, 11*(1), 121–136.

4
STEPPING BEHIND THE VEIL
A Methodology for Crafting a Loving Sanctuary

odo nyera

I'd lost myself
A wanderer within my own body
My life an amalgamation of
nomadic episodes,
where I extended pieces of myself
as gifts.
My heart was unevenly divided.
A portion offered to God. a sacrifice of faith.
A portion to my family;
a sacrifice of devotion.
One piece,
I retained for myself
To flame my desires
and feed my forward movement:
Along my journey,
other parts were stolen.
Harvested from my body
despite my cries against it.
When the body is raped,
the spirit survives;
until rebirth arrives.
So I walked this earth,
in ethereal form
until I stumbled upon my sisters.
They found me and (re)membered

> *Enhanced my essence*
> *with stories of power.*
> *Sang songs of praise*
> *They loved me into being*
> *until I could give birth to myself.*
> *Once reborn,*
> *they helped me (re)membered*
> *lessons of healing and passed them*
> *from open hands to my awaiting heart.*
> *Using threads from history,*
> *They mended my spirit and*
> *connected my past and present.*
> *Through my sister's eyes,*
> *I saw myself in a new light.*
> *I recognized beauty and deemed*
> *myself worthy.*
> *As such, I stood on my own two feet*
> *and tentatively took a step forward…*
> *As a collective my sisters stood and moved beside me.*
> *My journey forward would not be one of isolation,*
> *I would move with strength and dignity,*
> *not fearing the future*
> *because I know as I had known before…*
> *my sisters would be there*
> *to heal, love,*
> *celebrate, and support.*
> *I found myself in the sanctuary of sisterhood.*
>
> ~Dywanna Smith, 2018

In this chapter, I build from my story and anchor the stories of the Blue Diamonds to invite readers behind the veil of the Blue Diamonds' healing lessons to understand what we did as teachers, love advocates, and learners together. For those interested in a more detailed description of the methodology used to document and analyze the experience, those details are provided in the Appendix.

First, it is important to know the demographics in which the Blue Diamond experience occurred. Houston Middle School is in a primary city in South Carolina. At the time of the study (2015), South Carolina's population comprised 67% white, 26.5% Black, 2% Hispanic, and 1% Asian people (U.S. Census Bureau, 2019). South Carolina has a long-standing history of being mired in issues which have negatively impacted race and race relations including controversies over the Confederate Flag which flew over the statehouse capitol building from 1961 to 2015 (Holley & Brown, 2016) and ongoing incidents of racial profiling and brutality which include police officers detaining and in some cases murdering Black citizens simply because they were seen driving in predominantly white neighborhoods (Hawkins-Gaar & Duke, 2013). South Carolina is also the site of the Charleston Nine Massacre where nine innocent lives were taken while worshipping at the Mother Emanuel African Methodist Episcopal Church (Elliott, 2020). However, I want to be sure that the readers do not discount the stories in this book because they live in other states outside of "The South." The ongoing nature of Jim Crow attitudes and devastations *occur in every state in this country* as does the invalidation of Black girls in schools (Morris, 2019). Thus, the stories of myself and the young women in this study, are far from exclusive to South Carolina. They provide rich examples of African Americans dealing with race and racism and young women dealing with discrimination regarding gender, race, and size across the United States.

At the time of this study, the school district in which it was conducted enrolled 23,000 students from 41 countries. The district is geographically situated over 480 square miles and housed 28 elementary schools, nine middle schools, seven high schools, and eight specialty or charter schools. Its demographics included 73% African American, 19% white, and 8% students from other ethnicities. Seventy-three percent of the population participated in the free or reduced lunch program and 27% of the student population paid full price for their lunch.

The study was situated within Houston Middle School which housed students in the sixth through eighth grades. Its 2014 report card noted a school enrollment of 896 sixth-, seventh-, and eighth-grade students comprising 54.2% African American, 35.6% white, and 10.2% other ethnicities. At the time of the study, I worked with the local university serving as a professional development liaison to the school. Houston was a Professional Development School (PDS), its partnership with the local university allowing teaching interns to be placed with coaching teachers within the building and professional development to be provided for the school. As a liaison, I supervised the interns and provided professional development on school-selected topics. I had also previously worked at this middle school as a reading specialist and taught in the afterschool program for three years. Therefore, entering the study, I had a long-term established relationship with teachers, administrators, and students in the school.

Houston Middle School utilized an afterschool program in grades six to eight. The program operated on Tuesdays, Wednesdays, and Thursdays from 4:00 pm to 6:00 pm. Students entered the cafeteria at 4:00 pm to receive an evening meal. After their meal, students received homework assistance from the teachers. This occurred in a small group setting with teachers serving as content level specialists across grade-level bands. At 4:30 pm, students were released to their content- and grade-level-specific classes and remained with their instructors until dismissal at 5:55 pm. At this time, students were dismissed to their school buses or to meet awaiting parents/guardians.

FIGURE 4.1 Media Center Conference Room

The Blue Diamonds' Truth Circle

The five young women who were truth circle members met with me in Houston's Media Center Conference Room (see Figure 4.1) as a part of the tutorial element of the afterschool program. I planned and we engaged in a literature study that is detailed later in this chapter. The conference room was a private area situated within the school's media center which housed their professional development resources. The room featured a large oblong table and comfortable chairs which reclined or rocked. The table was large and offered group members space to spread out their belongings. The room had a large dry-erase board which we used to chronicle information such as charting group responses to journals and other texts. I selected this room for the reasons outlined above and arranged for our use of the room by speaking with Houston's media specialist. The door was always locked during truth circle meeting times and a sign hung outside the door to note that our truth circle was in session and should not be disturbed.

Truth Spaces Artifacts

The literature study was the foundation of our afterschool experience. Each week, the girls and I analyzed adolescent memoirs, popular music that discussed body images, photographs, and magazine images through informal spontaneous conversations as well as discussion questions I developed to facilitate our talk around each text (see Table 4.1 for a list of the texts and the discussion questions). Each text was chosen because it would provide an opening for us to interrogate race, gender, and size. By analyzing the intended message, observing, and reflecting on the presence or absence of stories, and sharing our own lived experiences, the research partners and I were able to examine converging social identities.

TABLE 4.1 Text Selection

Session	Texts	Discussion Questions
1: Body Size Images	Google images of adolescent girls from various body types including skinny, thick, and obese.	What words come to mind when you see her? What is her life like inside of school? What is her life like outside of school?
2: Social Media Analysis	Images from girl's social media pages	Why did you decide to post this image? What does it reveal about you? How do you decide what images to keep or delete on your social media pages?
3: Body Image Analysis: Race	Skin Tone Chart	Which tone do you find the most appealing? Why? Which do you find the most unattractive? Why? What issues or problems, if any, arise with skin tone? Explain.
4: Body Image Analysis	Body Image Scale	Which size do you find the most appealing? Why? Which size do you find the most unattractive? Why? What issues or problems, if any, arise with size? Explain.
5: Musical Analysis	"All About the Bass"	What does this song reveal about body image? Which line(s) reveal this? What does it reveal about race, gender, or size? What memories or experiences does the song provoke?
6: Magazine Analysis	Barbie Sports Illustrated Cover Nigerian Doll Article	What does this image/article reveal about body image? How do you know this? What does it reveal about race, gender, or size? What memories or experiences does the image/article provoke?
7 & 8: Literary Texts	Adolescent Obesity Memoir	What is the message of the story? How do you know this? What memories or experiences does the article provoke?
9 & 10: Body Image Collages	Google images selected by research partners	Why did you select the image(s)? What patterns or trends did you notice? What does this reveal about body image, race, or size?
11–15: Counter-narratives	Selected by research partners	Why did you select this style? What were the benefits? What were the disadvantages? How was the process of creating the counter-narrative? What does this reveal about body image, race, or size?

Each meeting of the Blue Diamond Truth Circle had a structured format. On day one, research partners introduced themselves by using a photograph and words to describe themselves. The girls created taxonomies or lists of introductions. The introductions included items such as names, favorite colors, number of siblings, favorite subjects in school, and favorite musicians. All girls admitted to hating reading and writing. The research partners then examined three pictures and wrote their "gut" reactions to three images of overweight or obese individuals. The pictures consisted of a fashionably skinny woman, a woman who is overweight but not by American standards, and an extremely obese teenager. Partners were instructed to annotate the images, explaining their reactions and how they imagined the person's life.

The remaining Blue Diamond Truth Circle meetings followed a similar structure. Each day, however, featured a new textual artifact. Members read and annotated textual artifacts. Research partners volunteered to lead the group discussion. All discussions were audiotaped and fully transcribed. The discussion was organic and pertained to research partners' interests and queries. Since the community was well-established and close-knit, all members spoke in every book discussion. Two questions were utilized to begin the discussion: (a) How did the text depict the overweight or obese individual, and (b) what tools or were utilized to describe or define the obese individual? I served as the facilitator using a semi-structured format. I wanted the opportunity to "delve deeper" into understanding the girls' experiences by being a part of the research process as not merely an observer, but a member and an observer.

Creating Counternarratives

As a part of our truth space, the research partners were charged with the task of creating counternarratives for girls struggling with pressures of race and size: love letters of affirmation. To begin this task, I asked the girls to reflect on ways in which we tell the stories of our lives. Their responses included songs, photographs, books, dance, and poetry.

Once each girl individually reflected, we began to discuss the benefits and disadvantages of each method. Afterward, the girls could select one or two methods to create a counternarrative from the aforementioned genres. Four days were provided in the media center for the research partners to brainstorm ideas about their selected methods before creating their own counternarratives. As the girls worked, I served as an archivist to write down ideas and take notes.

Journaling

Throughout our truth space, the research partners recorded their thoughts in journals. Each member was provided with a journal to collect their thoughts and insights on group activities. This allowed research partners to continue engaging with activities after the conclusion of each session by adding insights, comments, or questions as necessary, which they often did. It also allowed for research partners who are reluctant to speak out in the group in a less intimidating manner of participating. As adolescence is a period when young girls seek acceptance from their peers, the journal provided a contested space for members to reveal their innermost truths – a truth they may not have felt comfortable sharing with the entire group.

Research partners journaled on a weekly basis around topics I provided to support their reflections on their experiences as Black adolescent girls, discuss their definitions of body image, and describe the life of an obese adolescent as seen through their eyes. They also wrote about self-selected topics including dealing with anger when reprimanded in school and how to determine if your outfit has been slayed.

Journaling time occurred during the last 15 minutes of each truth space session. To help protect member privacy and confidentiality, when journals were not in use, they were locked inside of a file cabinet in my office. I was the only individual with a key to access the cabinet (Figure 4.2).

Supplies

During the first truth circle, each member was presented with a miniature suitcase containing a journal, ink pens, markers, and candy (see Figure 4.3) and were decorated by students. The suitcase contained a lock and provided an extra amount of security. I wanted everyone to feel welcomed to the community and wanted to demonstrate my commitment to learning from them. For this reason,

FIGURE 4.2 Journaling Supplies

FIGURE 4.3 Partners with Research Supplies

I shared notes from my research journal. Like the Blue Diamond Girls, my journal shared the same dates and topics but also included my personal insights and interpretations. I shared these selections because I hoped they demonstrated my commitment to loving transparency. I realized this was the case when the girls began to comment on my responses explaining what they enjoyed the most. This also allowed me to fact-check by asking the members about the interpretations.

Interviews and Other Data: Collection and Analysis

To understand the Blue Diamonds' experiences and my own, I used a variety of data collection methods (i.e., researcher's journal, interviews, group conversation transcriptions, photographs, and annotated artifacts). I observed and participated in the interactions of the group sessions to gain and be able to illustrate a clearer picture of how we each recognized, interpreted, and defined obesity. Throughout the study, I shared transcripts and my interpretations of data with the girls to ensure I captured their thoughts, ideas, inflections, and tones with as much integrity regarding their intent as possible. At the same time, my methodological stance includes an acknowledgment that no interpretation of another person's words can ever be "accurate" because words written or spoken in a moment may be interpreted differently, even by the author, in the next moment or another moment in time. However, this process allowed me to gain further insights into their experiences.

Interviews

Our ideas of obesity, race, and gender are socially constructed so interviews were important dialogic spaces that allowed research partners to verbally illustrate events and experiences they deemed to have significance to their understanding and construction of obesity, race, gender, and beauty (King, Horrocks, & Brooks, 2018). To obtain information regarding how students' interpreted ideals of beauty as represented in the media are interpreted and passed down from parents to their children's cultural interviews were utilized. Through these interviews, I was able to ask the students about "their memories, experiences, and understandings of events in their lives [using interviews as a] kind of a witnessing that challeng [ed] and counter [ed] 'the official story' document [ing] voices silenced and ignored by mainstream culture" (Glesne, 2016, pp. 103–104). Cultural interviews allowed the research partners to share their stories of how they learned their views of obesity.

Interviews were conducted at the beginning and end of a six-week research period using a semi-structured format. The same questions were utilized for the pre- and post-sessions. Interviews were scheduled to take place after school upon securing transportation for the students to be able to travel home afterward. Interviews were audio-recorded and transcribed for data analysis and coding. During the interviews, I also utilized a field journal (Schwandt, 2015) to triangulate (Denzin, 2016) data as well as take notes on emotional and nonverbal responses which are not detected by audio-only devices. Conducting these interviews at the beginning and end of the study allowed me to note growths and shifts in patterns of thought and served as a reflection and monitoring tool for members. The questions were developed to promote reflective thinking and help capture research partners' lived experiences:

- What comes to mind when you hear the words obese or fat? Why do you think you have those thoughts/feelings? Where and how do you think you learned them?
- What is it like being a Black adolescent girl? Can you think of examples?
- What are the expectations of Black adolescent girls in your home? In schools? In American society?
- What stigmas, if any, do you feel are associated with obesity or fat? Can you think of examples?
- What do you believe is society's ideal body size? Why do you think that? How did you come to this belief?
- What do you feel is your ideal body size? Do you feel there is a conflict between that ideal and society's ideal? Why or why not? Why do you think that? How did you come to this thought?
- What messages did you receive regarding body image and size? Who or what sent those messages? Where and how do you receive those messages?
- How do the media continue or stop body image and size tension? Give examples.
- Tell me a story about a time you have seen an obese or fat person in your life. How did you feel? How do you think that person felt? Why do you think you and the person felt that way?

- Do you think young people need assistance to deal with body and size issues in terms of identity? Should schools play a role? Why? Why not? How do you think schools can assist with body size and identity issues?

My Journal

Another critical element used to understand this experience was my own reflective journal and notes. The journal allowed me to describe my feelings and observations about conducting this kind of research. It added rigor to study as I recorded my own reactions, assumptions, expectations, and biases (Morrow & Smith, 2000). I recorded reflections in my journal daily. Reflections include my interpretive descriptions about the overall tone of the sessions, descriptions of the girls including body language and vocal tone, and questions which arose throughout the session. Capturing such thoughts also helped with data triangulation and member checking because they became pausing and reflection points which informed further questions I might ask the girls for clarification, ensuring the best that I could that their words were properly interpreted.

This journal was utilized to construct the auto-ethnographic – or autobiographical – sections of this work. As the research partners traversed through their journey of identity and awareness, their testimonies and stories served as markers and reminders of my own experience. When these moments occurred, I chronicled the memory and its catalyst into my journal which served to create an auto-ethnographic roadmap. Oftentimes when I reflected, my thoughts formed in typical sentence/narrative format. At times, my mind immediately directed me to write in a style in which I felt more comfortable: poetry. Therefore, my reflections comprised a range of formats including outlines, bulleted notes, lists, prose, and poetry. These formats were eventually combined to capture multiple elements and perspectives of the study experience which included my own.

Analysis

To analyze the data, I engaged in multiple coding cycles. As this study is informed by Critical Race Theory (CRT) and Black Feminist Thought, categories were established and color-coded for the CRT tenets of whiteness as Property, Racial Realism, and Intersectionalities as well as other categories. The remaining codes were created by reading and rereading data to construct patterns. Patterns were collapsed or expanded, as necessary. As I analyzed patterns, I realized that several of them revealed intersectionalities. For example, one of the research partners, Kelsey vividly described an encounter in which she was told by an administrator she must change her clothes because her body shape made her skirt too revealing. This was despite the fact her skirt length met the school's required standards. As this experience of racism involved gendered clothing and her naturally given attributes, it occurred at an intersection of gender, race, and body type. Such intersectionalities are denoted by asterisks. Throughout the analysis process, I would text or call the Blue Diamonds to see verify analyses. I learned with and from the Blue Diamond Girls throughout the entire research process (Table 4.2).

For another round of coding, I utilized In Vivo coding which is a process that allows researchers to describe whole ideas using specific words or phrases (Saldana, 2015). For example, when discussing struggles with obesity, Marie discussed an

TABLE 4.2 Descriptive Codes Used for Data Analysis

Descriptive Code

- Whiteness as Property
  - White Supremacy in Defining Beauty
- Describing white
  - Cultural Appropriation
  - Privilege
- Racial Realism
  - Internalized Racism*
  - Experiences with Racism*
  - Colorism*
  - Stereotypes/Stereotypical Images*
    - Race*
    - Gender*
    - Size*
- Describing Black
  - AAL*
  - Hair*
  - Culture*
- Body Dissatisfaction
  - Hair*
  - Skin tone*
  - Weight*
  - Size*
- Describing Fat
  - Perceptions*
  - Messages Regarding Fat*
  - Stigma and Violence*
- Resisting Oppressive Constructs
  - Asking for Assistance
  - Speaking Out
  - Seeking Community

* Stars have been used to denote intersectionalities.

example of what I interpreted to be (and labeled) *exclusionary* behavior. When describing relationships, this exchange between Marie and Amir took place:

MARIE: I wrote about desire because some people change their bodies to fit in. Yeah, sometimes if they are in a relationship and she's big.
AMIR: [co-narrating (Boutte, 2015), concluding Marie's thought] And he might not want her... He might not like it.

Based on my interpretation, the dual voices illustrated the concept of symbolic *exclusion* exemplifying the idea society, particularly adolescents, excludes the obese frame. The idea that boys or men will deny access to – exclude girls from – a relationship because of weight is voiced by two girls displaying adolescent conflict and tension. This allowed me to then identify and name other exclusionary examples throughout the data as I recognized how, for the Blue Diamond Girls, being obese and being popular rarely occurs (Reece, 2018). It is an example of how my coding strategies allowed me to connect the research partners' words and experiences (and my own) to the basic tenets of the study.

For the final round of coding, I employed emotional coding to capture how the research partners responded to obesity portrayals. Saldana (2015) argued that "since emotions are a universal human experience, our acknowledgement of them in our research provides deep insight into the members' perspectives, world views and life conditions" (p. 106). This can clearly be observed when Jennifer described how "the struggle is real" for obese and overweight adolescents by stating, "Fat people be struggling to put on their clothes. They struggle to put on their pants. ...Their clothes." For the selected excerpt, I inferred pity or empathy as Jennifer confessed to never having personal experience with these issues; and later corroborated my interpretation using member checking (Schwandt, 2015) by asking Jennifer to explain what she was feeling when she made that statement.

Positionality

During this study, there were many considerations of positionality – mine and the research partners. My position as a teacher and liaison, however, marked me as an outsider, and I was at first viewed as a spy garnering information for an administrative enemy (Glesne, 2016). This was not an interpretation. In fact, it was a question directly asked by Amir and Marie. This position changed as our community bonded and strengthened discussions and reading journal entries, particularly as I shared my own experiences and validated theirs. However, I recognize all my positions (adult, teacher, coach, and researcher, to name a few) come with power and privilege. Although members seemed comfortable enough to joke and reveal their stories, there was also a barrier because I am not a middle school student. My positioning as researcher and group member had both benefits and disadvantages. There was a difference in age between the Blue Diamond

Girls and me, as they were adolescents, and I was 37 years old at the time of the study. The age gap could have created a barrier for discussion. Yet, in my teaching experience, I have found that when students recognize that their opinions are appreciated and heard, they fully participate and extend themselves in critical discussions. As such, I did not position myself as an expert. Instead, I positioned myself as a learner, growing right beside them. I honestly shared my fears, questions, and insecurities. Once I demonstrated my willingness to be vulnerable, the girls welcomed me into the community.

In addition, my body size marked me both a group insider and an outsider. To the members who conformed to a thin ideal, my obese body could potentially be viewed from a range of biased views which could lead to a range of perceptions about me. To the members who self-identified as being obese or overweight, my body could be comforting, I could be a potential ally. Since body size is the nexus of my study, I needed to negotiate these conflicting perspectives and endeavored to create an environment in which my members were open and felt comfortable as they shared their stories. I believe such an environment was established by the sharing of personal family stories, tears openly shed, and hugs freely given. As a researcher, I navigated these shifting positions so I could acknowledge my own partial knowledge and the members' voices and expertise.

Presenting the Work: What You Need to Know About Ethnopoetry and Verse Novels

By now, readers have surmised that poetry is a significant analytic and representational tool in my work. Poems open each chapter. Poems play a significant role in the representation of my experiences in Chapter 1. And as you will see, poetry – *a novel in verse* – is the representation of the heart of this study – its findings – presented in Chapter 5. Thus, it is important that readers understand the rationale for using poetic methods. The analytic rigor behind the creation of each poem is detailed in Chapter 6.

What Is a Verse Novel?

A verse novel is a text which uses poetic form to convey a narrative story. In a speech at the Association of Writers and Writing Programs, Rita Dove, a former U.S. poet laureate, described how verse novels offer "the weight of each word, the weight of the sentence, the weight of the line, the weight of white space, heightened attention to sound, and deep allegiance to silence" (Dove, 2013). A well-crafted verse novel, "is pure energy/horizontally contained/between the mind of the poet/and the ear of the reader" (Giovanni, 1974). It is the combination of words, visual space, and attention to silence that creates an intimacy between the readers and the authors while providing a sense of urgency (Schneider, 2012). Verse novels mirror a culture's artistic, musical, and literary heritage while merging rhythm and melody to recreate the research partners' stories (Farrish, 2013). Combining artistry, printed word, and orality, verse novels build upon the rich Black Oral Tradition which celebrates performance, storytelling, verve, and communion (Boutte, 2015; King, 2005; King & Swartz, 2015). In essence, this genre is both a demand for space in which to invoke the art of storytelling and an invitation to critically listen with an open mind and a willing heart (Cadden, 2011).

The verse novel and its numerous intricacies reveal the ongoing tensions between words, voices, and roles; all of which must be manipulated to create a comprehensive. The goal of the verse novel is to provide a richer understanding of an event. As an added benefit, each component of the verse novel aids in the transparency of the research process because as Moravcsik (2013) argues, "Unless other scholars can examine evidence, parse the analysis, and understand the processes by which evidence and theories were chosen, why should they trust the research?" (p. 48).

Verse Novel as a Critical Act of Resistance

I also use the verse novel to challenge Eurocentric ways of presenting research in ways that invite my research partners and their peers as well as adults into the findings of this study. Black authors of adolescent literature have embraced and excelled in creating verse novels that draw readers in and inform, excite, move readers in powerful ways. Dean Atta's *The Black Flamingo* (2020), Elizabeth Acevedo's *The Poet X* (2018), and Jacqueline Woodson's *Brown Girl Dreaming* (2014) have won numerous awards for the compelling characters and gripping plots they portray through innovative use of the heart of the verse novel: an authentic and powerful voice. Verse novels also increased awareness of the power of the narrative voice and for "reading constructed as intimate conversation or even as eavesdropping... re-conceiv [ing] their narrative more explicitly as spoken text and oral rhythms assume greater significance (Alexander, 2014, pp. 270–271).

Through the verse novel, the research partners' stories from our truth space also construct a curriculum centered on students' realities and preferred forms of expression through co-generative dialogue, context, and content (Love, 2020).

The poems in this book are not only representational, but they are also a critical part of the analytic process as I weighed the Blue Diamonds' (and my own) words and experiences. Utilizing direct quotes from poetic transcription (Glesne, 2011) and combining the intentional use of pauses, line breaks, word choice, and positioning, we created the poems to bring what was once hidden to light; the pauses and line breaks providing hesitations necessary for reader reflection and action. In so doing, I was able to utilize the multitude of voices which comprised the data: the voices and stories of the Blue Diamond girls; my thoughts, experiences, and analyses as a researcher; current research; and the voices of writers, poets, photographers, as well as vocal and visual artists which comprise the Black literary ancestry. This action challenges hegemonic academic forces which hooks (hooks, 1990) argued are often predicated on the notion that there is no need

> To hear your voice when I can talk about you better than you can speak about yourself. No need to hear your voice. Only tell me about your pain. I want to know your story. And then I will tell it back to you in a new way. Tell it back to you in such a way that it has become mine, my own. Re-writing you I write myself anew. I am still author, authority… and you are now at the center of my talk.
>
> (p. 208)

Thus, our ethnopoetic findings constitute a purposeful and critical act of resistance because for far too long, the term "academic" has been relegated to white supremacist and colonized forms (Lyiscott, 20; Paris & Winn, 2014; Ohito, 2020). Smith (2012) pontificates about how research has long been known among the oppressed for its oppressive qualities:

> The word itself, 'research', is probably one of the dirtiest words in the indigenous world's vocabulary… it stirs up silence, it conjures up bad memories, it raises a smile that is knowing and distrustful. It is so powerful that indigenous people even write poetry about research. The ways in which scientific research is implicated in the worst excesses of colonialism remains a powerful remembered history.
>
> (p. 1)

In sum, the poems that constitute Chapter 5 are the result of rigorous data collection and analysis written to take readers into the lives and hearts of the Blue Diamonds. I present them without interruption refusing to diminish voices that have been silenced enough with commentary or explanation. I also made this choice because poetry cannot be gulped down. It should not be diluted or interrupted by excessive dissection. To fully internalize the words representing experiences, poetry must be sipped slowly and savored. I would like for readers to experience the poems by reading, pondering, and deeply reflecting on the themes of fat, colorism, intersectionalities, and counternarratives which unfold within them. Allow the poems to bear witness to the Blue Diamonds' realities, acknowledge our pain, and celebrate our resolve and growth. Read and reread to deepen your understanding. Allow an authenticity of the reading and interpretive experience, which is what all research is about anyway. Read these uninterrupted poems privileging the poetic voice as transformational steppingstones (hooks, 1990).

With both CRT and Black Feminist Theory to guide the appreciation of experiential knowledge, and counternarratives as liberatory spaces through which we might shake loose oppressive bonds (Bell, 1992; Collins, 2015; Cook, 2013), I offer Chapter 5 to help readers see and feel the need for spaces of Black girl sanctuary. Healing can only begin when we own our pain and share our stories (Lorde, 1990). I ask readers to read the poems to better understand why healing is necessary. Only then can we begin to think about transformation in schools. Read with critical eyes, listen with critical ears; and stand present before the text with an open and willing heart. I invite you to bear witness to our truths, our pains, and our triumphs.

References

Acevedo, E. (2018). *The poet X: A novel*. Harper Teen, an imprint of Harper Collins.
Alexander, K. (2014). *The crossover*. HMH Books.
Atta, D. (2020). *The Black Flamingo*. Balzer-Bray.
Bell, D. (1992). *Faces at the bottom of the well: The permanence of racism*. Basic Books.
Boutte, G. (2015). *Educating African American students: And how are the children?* Routledge.
Cadden, M. (2011). The verse novel and the question of genre. *The ALAN Review, 39*(1), 21–27.
Collins, P. H. (2015). *Black feminist thought: Knowledge, consciousness, and the politics of empowerment*. Routledge, Taylor & Francis Group.
Cook, D. A. (2013). Blurring the boundaries: The mechanics of creating composite characters. In M. Lynn & A. Dixson (Eds.), *Handbook of critical race theory in education: CRT and innovations in educational research methodologies* (pp. 181–194). Routledge.
Denzin, N. K., & Giardina, M. D. (2016). *Qualitative inquiry through a critical lens*. Routledge.
Dove, R. (2013). Staggered tellings: Immediacy, intimacy, and ellipses in the verse novel. Speech presented at Association of Writers and Writing Programs Conference in Hynes Convention Center, Boston, MA.
Elliott, D. (2020, June 17). 5 Years after Charleston Church Massacre, what have we learned? https://www.npr.org/2020/06/17/878828088/5-years-after-charleston-church-massacre-what-have-we-learned
Farrish, T. (2013). Why verse? Poetic novels for historical fiction, displacement stories, and struggling readers. *School Library Journal, 59*(11), 32–33.
Giovanni, N. (1974). *Poetry in my house*. Harper.
Glesne, C. (2011). *Becoming qualitative researchers: An introduction*. Pearson.
Glesne, C. (2016). *Becoming qualitative researchers: An introduction*. Pearson.
Hawkins-Gaar, K., & Duke, A. (2013, October 01). Hollywood couple stopped by police, say they were racially profiled. http://www.cnn.com/2013/09/30/showbiz/cherie-johnson-dennis-white-police-irpt/
Holley, P., & Brown, D. L. (2016, June 15). Woman takes down Confederate flag in front of South Carolina statehouse. Retrieved November, 2019, from https://www.washingtonpost.com/news/post-nation/wp/2015/06/27/woman-takes-down-confederate-flag-in-front-of-south-carolina-statehouse/
hooks, b. (1990). Marginality as site of resistance. In R. Ferguson, T. T. Minh-Ha, & C. West (Eds.), *Out there: Marginalization and contemporary cultures* (pp. 341–343). The New Museum of Contemporary Art.
King, J. E. (2005). *Black education: A transformative research and action agenda for the new century*. L. Erlbaum.

King, J. E., & Swartz, E. (2015). *The Afrocentric praxis of teaching for freedom: Connecting culture to learning*. Routledge.

King, N., Horrocks, C., & Brooks, J. M. (2018). *Interviews in qualitative research/Nigel King, Christine Horrocks, Joanna Brooks*. Sage Publications.

Lorde, A. (1990). *Need: A chorale for Black woman voices*. Kitchen Table: Women of Color Press.

Lyiscott, J. (2019). *Black appetite, white food: Issues of race, voice, and justice within and beyond the classroom*. Routledge, Taylor & Francis group.

Moravcsik, A. (2013). Transparency: The revolution in qualitative research. *Political Science & Politics APSC, 47*(01), 48–53.

Morris, M. W. (2019). *Sing a rhythm, dance a blues: Education for the liberation of Black and Brown girls*. The New Press.

Morrow, S. L., & Smith, M. L. (2000). Qualitative research for counseling psychology. In S. D. Brown & R. W. Lent (Eds.), *Handbook of counseling psychology* (3rd ed., pp. 199–230). Wiley.

Ohito, E. O. (2020). Fleshing out enactments of Whiteness in antiracist pedagogy: Snapshot of a White teacher educator's practice. *Pedagogy, Culture and Society, 28*(1), 17–36. https://doi.org/10.1080/14681366.2019.1585934

Paris, D., & Winn, M. T. (2014). *Humanizing research: Decolonizing qualitative inquiry with youth and communities*. SAGE Publications.

Reece, R. L. (2018). Coloring weight stigma: On race, colorism, weight stigma, and the failure of additive intersectionality. *Sociology of Race and Ethnicity, 5*(3), 388–400.

Saldana, J. (2015). *Coding manual for qualitative researchers*. Sage Publications.

Schneider, D. (2012, March). Poetry writing with novels in verse. *Book Links*, 20–22.

Schwandt, T. A. (2015). *The SAGE dictionary of qualitative inquiry*. Sage Publications.

Smith, L. T. (2012). *Decolonizing methodologies: Research and indigenous peoples* (2nd ed.). Zed Books.

U.S. Census Bureau. (2019, August). QuickFacts South Carolina. Retrieved November, 2021, from https://www.census.gov/quickfacts/SC

Woodson, J. (2014). *Brown girl dreaming*. Newberry.

5
POETIC JUSTICE
Truth Revealed in Verse

odo nyera

If I open my heart to you,
deftly display vulnerability
by making my soul
transparent
for your curious eyes,
will you change?
Or will you simply
collapse upon yourself
in guilty shame
and proclaim
yourself too fragile
to commit
to the hard work
transformation necessitates?
Will you be honest
and reply you are unwilling to change
because it would cause immeasurable pain
and you are far too comfortable
and far too complacent for change?
Will you critically peer
into your subconscious
and begin the tortuous

> process of uprooting
> white supremacy and
> patriarchy from
> your heart and mind
> where it has long
> since taken root?
> Will you reform
> your essence and
> your laws
> so, my body can
> Exhale?
> Exist?
> Expand?
>
> (Dywanna Smith, 2020)

Researcher's Note: Preface to the Novel

Can I really do this?
Can I bravely stand before five adolescent girls
pretending I'm fixed?
Declaring I'm healed
but knowing healing denotes recovery from injury.
My pain?
My pain is emotional trauma
and
physical assault.
My scars are but red bandages applied
to various positions on my body;
and though decades have passed,
they sometimes still pulse and feel raw.

Can I really do this?
Can I listen to their stories
and not fall back into the abyss of depression
from which I have crawled out?
Macabre nightmares;
Blood shedding;
Fingernails torn;
Bruised spirit …

but I'm fine.
Right?
Fixed?
Healed?
Confident?

Can I really do this?
Can I confront demons
I have locked into closets,
deep in the recesses
of my mind?
I've named each.
in an attempt to absorb their power.
And ... I feel stronger;
but even strength
can be but a dull dream
on which to cling.
So ....
Can I do this?
Can I really do this?

Introductions: A Poem in Five Stanzas

My name is ...
No! I am Amir!
Loud!
Crazy
and only 14!
I love boys, music ... anything that's green.
I am that tough girl everybody knows.
Big Mouth.
Big Personality.
Those stylish cornrows.
Step a little closer!
Come closer!
There's a secret I always hide.
I may seem quite confident,
but I hate myself on the inside.

Hi!
I'm Melody.

I don't know what you want me to say!
I really ... don't ... do this ... public speaking thing anyway.
I'm quiet.
Shy.
Yeah, I choose not to speak.
I'd rather listen, laugh, and watch the world ...
You know ...
be chill and meek.
I'm kind of use to hiding,
behind my eyes
and my smile.
But ...
If I really trust you, I'll let you in ...
at least, for a while.

Sup! I'm Kelsey!
Or would you rather I say, "Hello!"
I'm the confident chameleon;
shifting codes wherever I go.
When you see me, you best respect.
I know my stuff on fleek.
Boys love me.
Girls want to be me.
I'm cute! I'm beautiful! Stylish and chic!
Am I opinionated?
No.
I am just informed and knowledgeable.
Yes, baby, trust and believe ...
I share my wisdom wherever I go!

Hello. Jennifer, here!
How you want me to describe me?
My mama says I talk too much.
My teachers would say I'm mean.
You know what?
I'm not one thing or the other ...
At best, I'm in-between.
I'm the middle child.
I'm the second girl.
Not a baby but not an adult.
I just want someone to hear me ...

really see me.
I don't think that's asking too much!

Hey! I'm Marie.
Wha'cha want me to describe?
I'm me!
Plain and simple.
All truths.
Nothing to hide.
Straight up: I don't trust people.
That ish gets you hurt.
Some would say I'm rude …
Possibly I'm a little curt.
Speak my mind.
Never lie.
Got all this anger bottled up inside.
But I am quite loving, I ain't even gonna deny.
You hurt?
You need a hug?
I'll be happy to oblige!

Fat: A Definition Poem

[fat]
Adjective

1. an extension of identity;
2. a stigma;
3. a medical definition which marks an individual as "abnormal or different. By calling people 'overweight' or 'obese,' we are simply not delineating them by their body mass, but we are relegating them to the margins of society"[1];
4. a label which "becomes internalized by the 'overweight' or 'obese' who think that something is wrong with them or that they must change their behavior in order to meet a particular physical ideal"[2];
5. an acceptable form of prejudice, which encompasses "a system of damaging beliefs that pre-judge people – in this case, those with large bodies. Discrimination intensifies as weight increases, but size bigotry also affects those who are only 20% above their ideal weight"[3]
6. a site of resistance and love;

Synonyms: overweight; obese

Fat: A Visual Poem

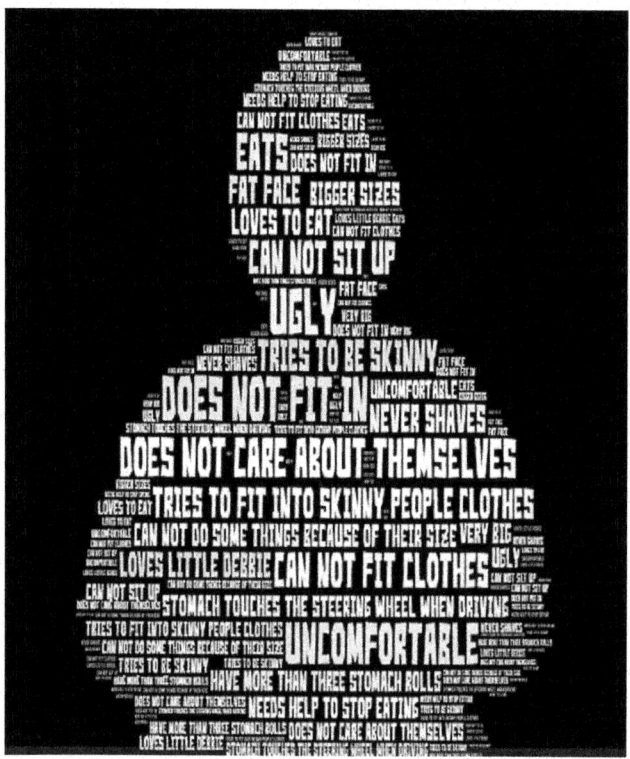

FAT: A Biography in Five Short Chapters

A Visual Poem

I.

II.

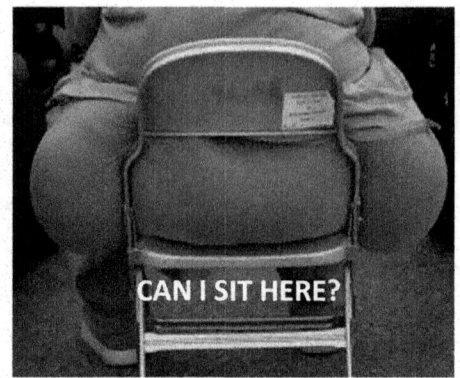

III.

IV.

V.

Stereotypes

I'm out of control.
Never had it
and I question
if I ever will.

I live my life
in **EXCESS**.
EXCESSIVE food.
Over-sized portions
which drip off of the plate.
Super-sized hamburgers
with triple … no quadruple patties.
Best believe I go from 0 to 100
real quick.
I straight flex on my food.

My stomach is **life-sized**!
Rolls upon rolls of fat.
I'm butter oozing everywhere.
I hemorrhage weight the
way others would blood.
It bypasses *the borders*
of my skirts

It peeks behind my blouses;
exposing the repugnance.
I need a bigger shirt!
I need a bigger everything.
Can someone stop feeding me?

STEP BACK!
I **NEED** space.
My smell may be
deemed offensive.
Besides, I need room to
BREATHE!
It's hard …
It's so hard …
taking in …
taking in …
air.
It's an ongoing
altercation between me
and the world.
It, like you,
must detest me.

I always try to
SQUEEZE…
well… fit into life.
Pulling clothes
over **bulbous
mounds**.
I want to
be stylish.
Fashion, like you,
ignores me.

I know you pity me.
It saddens me
but what can I do?
Moving is **torture**.
BREATHING is agony.
Living is **misery**.
I did this to myself.
I deserve no mercy.

I know it is
EASY
to lose weight.
I only need to
Stop **shoveling**
food in my mouth;
but I cling to my food
as I cling to my fat.
I need help.
Please!
Please ... help me!
I'm just so tired*!*

Fat: A Confessional

Spoken-Word Performance Poem

The stage opens with the spotlight shining on a metal chair: the confessional room of a popular reality television show. In the confessional room, the participants reveal their true feelings on any subject matter which they choose. The confessional room only requires complete honesty. To ensure honesty occurs, the room contains two items: a chair and a video camera.

A Black adolescent walks onto the stage and takes a seat in the chair. She stares straight into the audience looking into it as if it is her mirror. She takes lipstick from her pocket and gently glides it over her lips. She makes kissy faces at the audience and tilts her head back and forth as she fluffs her afro-puffs. The girl reaches over with her hand and makes a motion to switch on the video camera. When she speaks, it is with a clear, loud, and confident voice.

> Is this thing on?
> Is this thing on?
> How am I looking?
> Um! Girl, you look good!
> Looking sexy!
> What am I 'posed to be doing?
> What am I 'posed to be talking about again?
> Oh, yeah!
> You want me to talk about those big girls in middle school.
> Being fat in middle school... it ain't easy.
> It's tough.
> Straight difficult;
> an emotional roller coaster.
> It's confusing because

you ain't one thing or the other.
You ain't on people's radar;
yet, somehow you always there.
People know your every move.
You ain't got no secrets.
Chile… fat can't have secrets.
It's all out in the public for everyone to see.
You get watched because you are a show.
A sadistic reality show…
Comedy and tragedy rolled into one.
People laugh at you.
You always the butt of someone's joke.
HA!
Now that's funny … the BIIIIGGGG butt of someone's joke!
People just glare at you in the hallways.
Staring at you as you grow outside your clothes.
You must upset your parents with all that growing.
nobody got time to keep buying you clothes.
It's too expensive.
They laugh at you.
They laugh at the fat.
They laugh at …
They just laugh.
People point at you on the stairwells.
Push you up over each rise because they want to "help."
"Help!"
HA!
More like "help" push you to your limits.
They listen to your ragged breaths as you push your bulk forward.
It's not normal… exhaling like that.
Every breath a moment's recording … a staccato tempo of death.
Someone should help;
provide an escalator or something.
We got an elevator but being that fat ain't no disability…
is it?
Keepin' it 100… everyone pities you;
gawk at you barely able to move… to do simple things like walking.
It's sad… depressin' really.
At lunch, it's worse.
The entire event is a performance.
Everyone stops to watch them shovel in junk food…

Chicken wings…
Burgers…
Cookies…
It's repulsive!
Being fat in middle school… it ain't easy.
It's tough.
Straight difficult;
an emotional rollercoaster.
They laugh at you.
They laugh at the fat.
They laugh at …
They just laugh.
Guess I shouldn't have said all that.
But they the ones said they wanted the truth.
And what I said honey … that is straight truth.

(She reaches over to turn the camera off, makes one last kissy face at the audience, stands up and walks confidently off the stage.)

Researcher's Note: The Skinny on Fat

What is it about fat that makes society hate it so much?
Is it the extra pounds which surround bodies?
Is it the images of excess?
Is it the increased revenue which emerges from a war on weight?
I pondered this question as a child, adolescent, and
it still lingers as an adult.
I came to this topic hoping for insight;
hoping adolescent truth would garner new wisdoms.
As we journeyed together, I realized…
my girls were just as confused about fat as I.
While we talked, they ruminated on health.
One cannot be fat and healthy
It was too far-fetched an idea to contemplate.
One thing was clear: fat created a distance.
It provided a divide in its owner:
One of love and hate.
It created a divide in the casual observer
because they did not know how to respond.
Should I despise?
Should I laugh at it?

Should I pity it?
Can I ... love it?
Can a person possibly love their fat?
Even more, this feeling of uncertainty,
of not knowing how to react to fat,
endured into the very last meeting.
During our sessions...
No, during our confessionals...
adolescent minds contemplated this complex topic.
Some of their girls loved their curves.
Others denied them.
I observed and listened.
I wiped away tears.
I gave hugs to heal painful scars.
I praised confidence and self-love... and I realized...
This is what we need to combat the hate surrounding fat:
a contested space within the walls of schools to speak our minds;
to discuss our realities;
to ponder our confusions.
Solutions never come quickly,
but resolve can be found with time.
If a space can be offered,
perhaps we can finally get the skinny on fat.

Colorism: A Definition Poem

Col/or/ism
/kələrˌizəm/
Noun

1. Coined by author Alice Walker in 1982, colorism is "the prejudicial treatment of individuals falling within the same racial group on the basis of skin color"[4];
2. "A hierarchically based skin tone bias, one that poses a psychological obstacle for
    a. various racial groups, specifically with regard to variances within racial groups"[5];
3. "A process that privileges light-skinned people of Color over dark in areas such as
    a. income, education, housing, beauty, and the marriage market"[6];

b. For example, in education, "students of Color who have lighter skin could have access to increased social capital that can convert into educational and economic capital"[7];
4. Colorism's roots are "located in the European colonial project plantation, life for enslaved African-Americans, and the early class hierarchies of Asia. Despite its disparate roots, today, colorism in the USA is broadly maintained by a system of white supremacy"[8];
5. Emotional terrorism which can potentially block self-actualization.

The Color Complex: An Introduction

A Black Out Poem

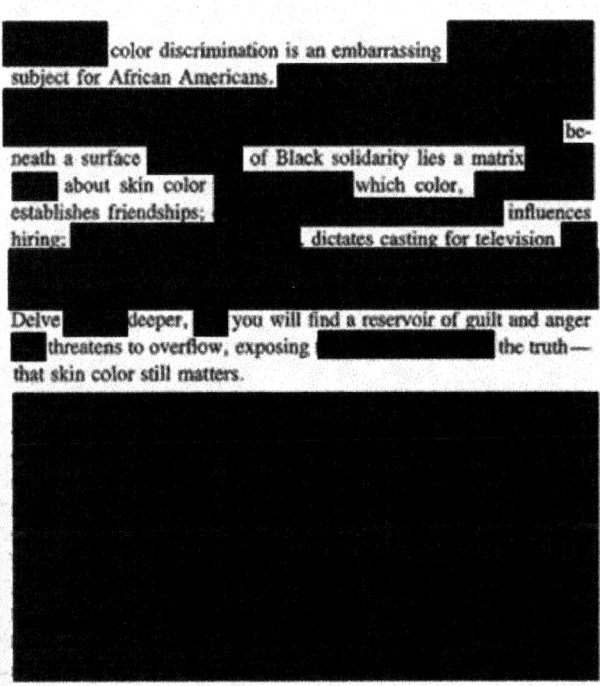

Too many blackfolks are fools about color and hair.

color discrimination is an embarrassing subject for African Americans.

be-
neath a surface   of Black solidarity lies a matrix
        about skin color   which color,
establishes friendships;   influences
hiring;   dictates casting for television

Delve   deeper,   you will find a reservoir of guilt and anger
     threatens to overflow, exposing   the truth—
that skin color still matters.

Dark Girls: A Poem in Two Voices

Can dark skin be beautiful?

No!		Of course!
	What? How can you say that?	
Dark skin and I mean real, dark skin…Dark skin, like mine, is the least attractive.		
		No! Black is always beautiful! It's just the way we are!
	Dark skin is…	
Hideous!		Sexy!
	What? How can you say that?	
No one can see if you are too dark!		
		Dark skin with chocolate brown eyes… Girl, Please! It's just pure sexy!
	If you have dark skin people think…	
you African or say you are from Haiti.		
		What's wrong with that? All I'm hearing you say is that there are different types of Black beauty.
	The perfect skin tone is…	
Light and bright. You know…Melody's color. That skin tone always gets more attention and more boys.		
		What? Dark girls get boys too! I'm dark and I can get any boy I want.
	But light skin does have its perks. Light-skinned students do get treated better in classes. Like Christian.	

(Continued)

He can do anything!		
And nothing happens! They just look at him and say, "Now, now! You know better!"		Talk back to teachers.
	Yeah. Light-skin does have its perks but dark skin is …	
Black and ugly. I'm sick and tired of the color Black. It's just too dark.		
		But that's who we are. It's my skin tone and it's your skin tone. You are…
Hideous!		Beautiful!

Heart's Desire: Colorism in Action

I don't want no dark skin boys!
I really think a light-skinned guy is the best!
A light-skinned guy.
You know the type… mulatto colored.
They act right.
They act better.
Light-skinned boys lick their lips and it's really sexy.
A dark-skinned boy does that and it's just like…
"What are you doin' son?"
I ain't never seen a light-skinned boy who didn't look good.
Perfect faces with their hair slick down.
They walk into a room like they own it.
But I…
I don't even want a light-skinned guy.
I want a white man.
They say if you marry a white man, then…
your baby's eyes will be blue.
So, I am gonna marry a white man…
And I …
I
  will
    have
      a
        light-skinned

>   baby
>   with
>   pretty
>   blue
>   eyes.

Researcher's Note: Delving into Skin

My mother's skin,
like her mother before her,
and her mother before,
is reminiscient of Gabon Ebony.
darker than the midnight sky;
deeper than oblivion;
revealing an uncomprising strength;
an unmitigated joy;
When polished its surface
becomes a mirror
reflecting her elegance
and beauty.

My father's skin,
like his father before him,
and his father before,
evokes the fruit
from the cacao tree.
Enriched by the fertile earth;
drenched in the sun's rays,
absorbing its essence
until it matures into perfection:
An aged and weathered copper.
One that is malleable to change
and radiates power.

My skin blends ebony and copper
creating a composite of color;
my patchwork quilt of beauty.
Part cinnamon,
part carob.
Affectionately labeled
pecan tan by my grandma.
Though I now love it,
and revel its its exquisteness;

as an adolescent,
I loathed it.
Desired to change it,
I wanted to bleach it pure;
Dissolving the darkest melanin
Until only alabaster beauty remained.

I'd internalized
That "white is Right,"
but light was still acceptable.
And if I was neither,
then I was
nothing.
Simply put, I was
colorstruck.
Blinded by a complex,
compliation of
Western values.
It blocked my acctualization
and imprisoned me in my skin.
It would take years
of affirmations
and soul-searching
before I would
free myself of those
confining ideals;
Shedding hate
and embracing love.

But…
that was my sojourn into being.
It had to be better today.
Decades have passed.
My story predates the
"My Black is beautiful" and
"Pretty Brown Girls" Movements.
My story predates Lupita Nyong'o
being heralded for her beauty.
It just had to be better today.
I foolishly clung to my
optimism as a security blanket;
hoping that these five girls'
identity quest,

partiularly race and skin tone,
would be easier than mine.
Yet, as I faced their truths,
and bore witness to their stories,
I grimly realized,
These girls... my girls...
were also colorstruck.

A generation may have passed,
but the legacy of colorism endured.

Intersectionality: A Definition Poem

In/ter/sec/tion/al/ity
/ intərsekSHəˈnalədē/
Noun

1. Coined by legal scholar Kimberle` Crenshaw, intersectionality emerged from CRT and analyzes the "multidimensionality of marginalized subjects' lived experiences"[9];
2. Interprets the "various ways in which race and gender interact to shape the multiple dimensions of Black women's ... experiences"[10];
3. Embraced by both CRT and Black feminist scholars;
4. Multi-faceted and serves several purposes:
   a. Challenges the race/gender binaries most often used in identity politics
   b. provides a vocabulary to challenge the dominant ideology
   c. provides a framework for recognizing and acknowledging exclusionary practices used to analyze lived experiences of Black women[11];
5. Expanded to include "the relationship among multiple dimensions and modalities of social relations and subject formations"[12];
6. A lens which to better study and understand the politics of survival for Black girls.

A Tale of Two Girls: Life as a Black Girl

You!
Hey, you!
Are you listening to me?
You want to know what is like
being a Black girl in
middle school?
At this school?
Fine!

I'll tell you but
you ain't gonna like it.
Let's call this…
A tale of two girls.

So, it was this Black girl.
She don't go to this
school anymore but
I ain't gonna speak her name.
And it was this white girl.
The white girl,
she was passing
the Black girl in the hallway,
but had to stop.
A bunch of boys
surrounded the Black girl.
You know… she was kind of cute.
Ain't nothing was wrong with her.

Now, the Black girl, she don't like what the
boys are doing.
She's telling the boys
to back off.
She ain't trying to
draw no attention
to what's happening.
She trying to
handle it herself
and keep it quiet,
but it doesn't work.
She looks around for help
and makes eye contact with
guess who?
Yup! The white Girl.

She looks this Black girl
in her eyes.
She saw the
fear on her face.
She watched as these boys
try to rub their hands
on the Black girl's butt.

Trying to touch it like they own it.
I mean the
boys were trying
to assault her.
The white girl
observes all of this
and do you know
what she did?
She turned her back
and walked away.

That's bad enough right?
But, it doesn't end there.
The Black girl fights and
breaks free of the boys.
She calmly walks
to her math class.
Guess what?
You know it!
She's in the same class
as the white girl.
Sits right beside
her EVERY day.
EVERY day!
I'm sitting behind them,
watching all this
foolishness play out.

Now, this is an
honors class
so ain't no
dummies here.
The teacher is
going on about something
and the Black girl, she
misses something.
She looks at the
white girl and she says,
"I did not get the answer
to number four and I
left my notes in my locker."
She sounded real sophisticated.

Once again, she was asking
the white girl for help.
That white girl looked at her
and was like, "I don't know either."
She ain't tried to help her.
AGAIN!
You could tell by the
way she was looking
at the Black girl like ...
like...
she ... was ignoring her;
just like she ignored
what happened
in the hallway.
She was
just a bystander
to the Black girl's
pain.

I told you,
you wasn't gonna like it.
I told you,
it wouldn't be pretty; but life never is
for a Black girl
at this school.

Remixed: Countee Cullen's Experience in 2015

Once while walking down a middle-school hallway,
Joyous heart and content as could be,
I saw a fellow middle school student
boldly staring almost challenging me.

Now, I am a knowledgeable 8th grader
and she was not smarter nor bigger,
She said not one word of compassion.
Instead, glared and called me, "Nigger!"

I saw humanity's cruelty that day
My pride she hoped I'd surrender.
Of all the things I learned that year,
That is the only lesson I remember.

I walked away both shock and saddened;
Bruised heart and spirit torn uncontrollably,
I did not share my pain with one teacher,
because why would they believe me?[13]

Enabling the System: A Cry for Help Denied

How many times?
How many times?
<u>How many times?</u>
I've told teachers.
I've told counselors.
You still don't do nothing.
You don't even care.
You know what…
My voice grows hoarse from asking the words:
How many times?
How many times do I ask for your help and you ignore me?
You just walk away or give me some sort nonsense about life not being fair.
You look at me and see and child and think… she can't even understand.
But you don't get it.
I was born black and a girl.
I learned that life is not fair before I could clearly say my name.
I learned that life is not fair when you don't respond when I cry, "Help me!"
I learned that life is not fair when I have to work three times as hard to get your attention.
That takes me back to my point.
How many times will you see me in pain and close the door on my face?
I just want equity.
I repeatedly remind you that you ain't even right.
You respond to my pain by telling me that I am being rude or defiant.
Defiant?
How can I be defiant by asking you to just see me?
How can I be defiant when I am simply asking you for help?
How can I be defiant when you, my teacher, refuse to fight for me?
How can I be defiant for asking you to care?
Because I best not ask for anything more.
I didn't realize that genuine love is offensive,
But then again…
How many times have you shown me that it is?

A Pocket Full of Wishes: Attracting the Opposite Sex

    I wish…
        I wish…
            I wish…
    I wish my thighs were thicker.
    I wish my butt was bigger.
    I wish my my skin was lighter.
    I wish my smile was brighter.
    I wish I could capture your heart
    and be everything you need.
        But….
    If I'm all of those things, would I still be me?

What Is Body Image?

    What is body image?
    It's how I see myself when I look in the mirror.
    Short.
    Tall.
    Over-weight.
    Small.
    It's how I picture myself in my mind.

    What is body image?
    It's how I see myself when I look in the mirror.
    It encompasses all.
    Hair color
    and length.
    Eyes.
    Skin tone.
    Even a smile.
    It's how I picture myself in my mind.

    What is body image?
    It's how I see myself when I look in the mirror.
    It's authentic;
    can't be faked.
    Though it may change,
    from day to day.
    A dynamic,
    moving force;

which shifts
and moves
as I alter my course.
It's how I picture myself in my mind.

What is body image?
It's how I see myself when I look in the mirror.
All the words and
images that construct who I am.
Beautiful.
Bold.
Or hideous to behold.
It's how I picture myself in my mind.

Blessings upon Blessings: The Body as a Source of Conflict

I can't help it that
when God was passing out
blessings he granted
me extra favor in some
areas of my body.
I'm proud of
who I am.
When I come to
school, however,
you want me
toss my pride
aside
and exist
in your
world of ups
and downs.
You know:
Shut up!
Cover up!
Sit down!
Back down?
Never that.
I was not
made to hide.

Despite their
confusing nature,

I follow all your rules!
When I wear skirts,
they are long enough to reach
my fingertips.
Don't believe me?
Then ask my mama!
She checks everyday
before I walk out
the door.
I almost always seem
to make her approval;
but somehow,
I never can get yours.

I walk down the
hallways like
it's a runway.
Hair and outfit
on fleek.
You take one
passing glance
at my outfit
Don't even say,
"Good Morning,"
or "Hello."
You just give me two
options:
Put on some
long, old, T-Shirt
or
Call my mom
to bring a change of
clothes.

The reason
you want me
to cover up
and shut up is
because my
skirt rises
in the back
when I walk.
So, now it's not

just my clothes
that are offensive.
It's me.

I can't change
that.
Can't remove
my assets and
wouldn't if I could.
So I begin to
fight this
war.
It's a war
you started
because I … I
wanted to learn
I choose option two.
I call my mother
and she refuses to
bring me
clothes because
I was respectfully dressed
for her house;
just not for yours.
But does that matter?
No!
No one asks me
how I feel.
No one
wants to
hear my voice.
My refusal
is coded
as "disruptive
behavior,"
and I
am sent
to in-school
suspension.

I have to sit there
all day

because
I'm blessed
and highly favored.
Missing lessons.
Missing friends.
Missing my teachers.
Missing what
truly matters.

I seethe
all day
knowing this is
injustice in a simpler form.
The bell rings.
The day ends
and I walk
out from the
shadows.
What do I see?
My principal.
The same
woman who
banished me
without saying hello,
complimenting
dear, sweet,
white, Mary Alice
on her outfit.

I stare at
Mary Alice's clothes
and I rage
because we are
practically wearing
the same thing.
Only her skirt doesn't
ride up it just sits
there on her thin frame.

I'm confused!
I'm livid!
What the hell

do you want me
to do?
Trim down my ass?
Bind my breasts?
Would that be enough?
Would it be enough for you?
No! It won't!
Let's face it!
In your eyes,
I'll never be acceptable.
My skirts will always be too short.
My tops just a tad too tight.
See, I'm almost close …
But never … Never right!

I know we will
battle again
soon;
and once again
I'll be sent
to in –school.
Honestly,
I'd rather
stay there
and be true
to myself
then to give
in and appease
your injust
requests.
You see…
I refuse to stop.
I refuse to change.

Researcher's Note: Examining Intersectionalities

Identity is a complex thing.
To analyze it, we must
first begin with the whole;
the totality of being.

The culmination of
memories, experiences, and knowledge.
It is this which forms our shape.
Still, we are not simply the sum of all those things,
because the whole is comprised
of separate yet equally relevant pieces,
Race.
Gender.
Size.
Religion.
Age.
Sexuality.
Along with many others.
It is the amalgamation of these things
which form our substance.
Sometimes still, these fragments
will converge and align
in such a way
that a new form
of examination
can take place.
Intersectionalities.
Our core
is made up
these powerful
yet often
overlooked junctures.

I wanted to delve
deeper into the
intersections of adolescence:
when race, gender, and
body image intersect.
I asked my girls
to speak truths
about questions
which may
be seldom asked
in schools.
What is it like being a Black girl

in middle school?
What have you encountered
because of your race and gender?
What have you experienced
because of your race,
gender, and size?
My inquiry was not cautious;
and neither were their responses.
I heard their rage.
I heard their sadness.
I heard their doubt.
I also heard a staunch
resistance to conform
to that which was not right.
At the end, I was
awed, outraged, and proud.
Afterwards, I applauded
our mutual honesty.
Without missing a beat,
they each thanked me
for be willing
to ask difficult questions.

Counternarratives: A Definition Poem

coun·ter •nar·ra·tive
'koun (t)ər/'nerədiv/
Noun

1) A powerful pedagogical tool to "challenge majoritarian stories rooted in a dominant Eurocentric perspective that justify social inequities and normalize white superiority and thus, white supremacy"[14];
2) "A method of telling the stories of those people whose experiences are not often told"[15];
   a. Examples include Derrick Bell's *Faces at the Bottom of the Well* (1992)[16] and Richard Delgado's *Rodrigo's Chronicles* (1995)[17];
3) Types of Counternarratives:
   a. Personal Stories;
   b. Other People's Stories;
   c. Composite Stories[18];

4) Purposes:
   a. Build and sustain a community for people often marginalized and overlooked;
   b. Critique/challenge commonly held ideas or notions;
   c. Create a new perspective into reality; open possibilities;
   d. Combine current reality with open possibilities to create a new rich world[19];
5) A mirror revealing one's true self;

Naming Myself: A Body Image Visual Poem

Fat: A Counternarrative in Visual Form

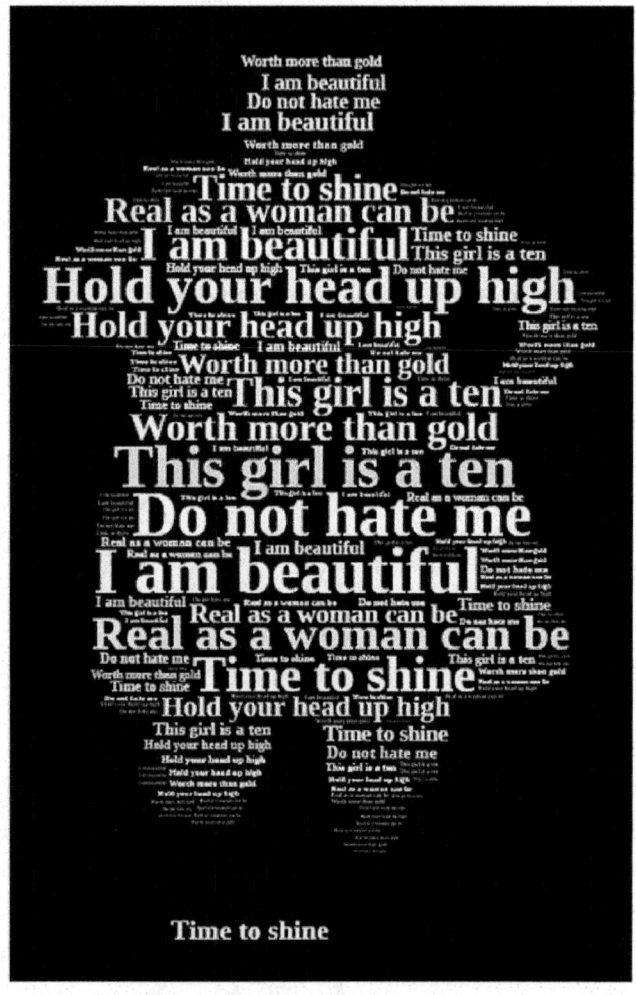

Greater is Coming: Praise in Lyrics and Movement

Body Love: An Autobiography in Five Short Chapters

A Visual Poem

I. Respect All Bodies!

II. Know Your Worth!

III. Live Your Life Without Negative Thoughts!

IV. Be at peace!

V. Love Yourself

Notes

1. Oliver, J. E. (2006). *Fat politics: The real story behind America's obesity epidemic*. Oxford University Press
2. Taylor, S. R. (2018). *The body is not an apology: The power of radical self-love*. Berrett-Koehler.
3. Cox, J. (2020). *Fat girls in black bodies: Creating communities of our own*. North Atlantic Books.
4. Woodson, K. M. (2020). *Colorism: Investigating a global phenomenon*. Fielding University Press.
5. Mcgee, E. O., Alvarez, A., & Milner, H. R. (2015). Colorism as a salient space for understanding in teacher preparation. *Theory into Practice, 55*(1), 73.
6. Hunter, M. (2007). The persistent problem of colorism: Skin tone, status, and inequality. *Sociology Compass, 1*(1), 237.
7. Mcgee, E. O., Alvarez, A., & Milner, H. R. (2015). Colorism as a salient space for understanding in teacher preparation. *Theory into Practice, 55*(1), 75.
8. Russell-Cole, K., Wilson, M., & Hall, R. E. (2013). *The color complex: The politics of skin color in a new millennium*. Anchor Books.
9. Crenshaw, K. (1989). Demarginalizing the intersection of race and sex: A Black feminist critique of antidiscrimination doctrine, feminist theory and antiracist politics. *The University of Chicago Legal Forum*, 139.
10. Crenshaw, K. (1991). Mapping the margins: Intersectionality, identity politics, and violence against women of color. *Stanford Law Review, 43*(6), 1244.
11. Nash, J. C. (2008). Re-thinking intersectionality. *Feminist Review, 89*(1), 1–15.
12. McCall, L. (2005). The complexity of intersectionality. *Signs: Journal of Women in Culture and Society, 30*(31), 1771.
13. Cullen, C. (2013). *Collected poems*. Amistad Research Center.
14. Huber, L. (2008). Building critical race methodologies in educational research: A research note on critical race testimonio. *FIU Law Review, 4*(1), 167.
15. Solorzano, D. G., & Yosso, T. J. (2002). Critical race methodology: Counter-story telling as an analytical framework for education. *Qualitative Inquiry, 8*(1), 26.
16. Bell, D. (1992). *Faces at the bottom of the well: The permanence of racism*. Basic Books.
17. Delgado, R. (1995). *The Rodrigo chronicles: Conversations about America and race*. NYU Press.
18. Delgado, R., & Stefancic, J. (2001). *Critical race theory: An introduction*. NYU Press.
19. Delgado, R. (2014). *Critical race theory an introduction* (2nd Ed.). NYU Press.

References

Bell, D. (1992). *Faces at the bottom of the well: The permanence of racism*. Basic Books.
Crenshaw, K. (1989). Demarginalizing the intersection of race and sex: A Blackfeminist critique of antidiscrimination doctrine, feminist theory and antiracist politics. *The University of Chicago Legal Forum*, 139.
Crenshaw, K. (1991). Mapping the margins: Intersectionality, identity politics, and violence against women of color. *Stanford Law Review, 43*(6), 1244
Cullen, C. (2013). *Collected poems*. Amistad Research Center.
Delgado, R. (1995). *The Rodrigo chronicles: Conversations about America and race*. New York University Press.
Delgado, R. (2014). *Critical race theory: An introduction* (2nd ed.). NYU Press.
Delgado, R., & Stefancic, J. (2001). *Critical race theory: An introduction*. New York UniversityPress.
Huber, L. (2008). Building critical race methodologies in educational research: A research note on critical race testimonio. *FIU Law Review, 4*(1).

Hunter, M. (2007). The persistent problem of colorism: Skin tone, status, and inequality. *Sociology Compass, 1*(1), 237.

McCall, L. (2005). The complexity of intersectionality. *Signs: Journal of Women In Culture and Society, 30* (31), 1771.

McGee, E. O., Alvarez, A., & Milner, H. R. (2015). Colorism as a salient space for understanding in teacher preparation. *Theory into Practice, 55*(1), 73.

Nash, J. C. (2008). Re-thinking intersectionality. *Feminist Review, 89*(1), 1–15.

Oliver, J. E. (2006). *Fat politics: The real story behind America's obesity epidemic*. Oxford University Press.

Russell-Cole, K., Wilson, M., & Hall, R. E. (2013). *The color complex: The politics of skin color in a new millennium*. Anchor Books.

Solorzano, D. G., & Yosso, T. J. (2002). Critical race methodology: Counter-Story telling as an analytical framework for education. *Qualitative Inquiry, 8*(1), 26.

6
YOU CAN'T HEAL WHAT YOU DON'T REVEAL

Ethnopoetics as Truth, Resilience, and Resistance

odo nyera

JOURNEY INTO ME

It takes courage to critically analyze self.
To ask yourself to reflect upon
your beliefs, judgments, and perceptions.
Ideals held staunchly for a lifetime.
Writing this manuscript has been a journey into me.
Combing through the abyss of my life.
Navigating chaos.
Drowning in fear.
Seeing the world through broken lenses.
Recognizing that perceptions are often distorted.
Understanding there are many truths.
Wrapping oneself in the comfort of
not knowing.
Embracing multiplicity of ideas.
Loving stories.
Sharing your heart with others.
Naming power and privilege.
Erasing silence and marginalization.
Through conversations, distorted visions are cleared.
Once staunch-held beliefs are discarded
and fall away
as autumns leaves.
You realize…
you are NOT a chameleon

> *blending into dominant ideals.*
> *You are an art form.*
> *A softly drawn, water colored Sankofa bird.*
> *One whose bright colors stand against*
> *the starkness of ignorance.*
> *Confidently, you spread your wings and take flight*
> *Impassioned, you seek to touch lives,*
> *just as yours was touched.*
> *Realizing this is not the end,*
> *only the first of many new beginnings.*
> *To reflect.*
> *To act.*
> *To engage in praxis.*
> *Flying on the wings of change.*
>
> Dywanna Smith, 2016

As I approached the task of writing the poetic findings that constitute Chapter 5, I was intrepid. How would I bring the chorus of voices – my own and the voices of the young women in our truth space – together into a seamless but poignant story? It would need a structure to make it cohesive; yet the structure could not temper the emotional cacophony which imbued every session as adolescents wrestled with dealing with life in the margins and multifaceted intersections. It was in her speech "Learning from the 60s" that Audre Lorde (1984) declared, "There is no thing as a single-issue struggle because we do not live single-issue lives." Analyzing the perceptions of African American adolescent girls could not be a single issue as it is far more complex. Critically analyzing racism, sexism, and sizism demanded multiple perspectives.

It was essential that I find a way to communicate findings from our truth space in a way which rejoiced in Blackness, Black Intellectual Thought, and Black Feminist Thought. As described in detail in this chapter, the poems are the result of intensive and intentional data analysis, written as a blatant refusal to be ignored, overlooked, or silenced.

Organizing the Poems and Analytic Decisions

The cohesion of the poems that are Chapter 5 is built on a common structure. I did not explain this structure prior to presenting the findings poems because I felt that the poems and their organization must speak for themselves. Knowing that, no matter the format or style of texts, as readers transact with them, every interpretation becomes, in and of itself, the creation of a new poem (Rosenblatt, 1978). However, here I offer my thinking as I used analyzed data to construct the interpretations which became Chapter 5.

Within the first few pages, readers are introduced to an anxious researcher and five enthusiastic and energetic adolescent girls. The remainder of the novel is comprised of four distinct yet interconnected trend chapters discussing fat, colorism, intersectionality, and counternarratives. Each trend chapter begins with a poem of definition which utilizes current research to provide context and interject ideas and transform established beliefs and ideology (Solorzano & Yosso, 2001).

Following the poems of definition, composite poems are employed to speak to the girls' realities and convey my interpretations of their stories. Composite poetry builds upon the idea of composite characters in Critical Race Theory (CRT) (Bell, 1992; Cook, 2013) and Black Feminism (Griffin, 2016) which capture the breadth and depth of the issue while providing a closer lens to analyze the minute nuances at play. The composite poems were created using the partners' personal experiences, stories, and worldly observations (Cook, 2013) taken from journals, artifacts, and audio recordings. The result is what Bell (1992) described as modular stories or stories which are "composed as a mosaic, a design made up of component parts: What modular design can do is liberate the writer from linear logic, those chains of cause and effect, strings of dominoes always falling forward" (p. 158).

Composite poems allow the reader to experience a reality versus solely reading it. In essence, the composite poems serve as counternarratives to dominant research practices as they can (a) construct communal bonds for marginalized individuals by putting a human face on societal issues; (b) challenge majoritarian values and beliefs; (c) open doors to new possibilities by displaying "you are not alone"; and (d) instruct using narrative story elements to reveal the current reality (Solorzano & Yosso, 2001). The poems also celebrate Black joy and creativity as they are modeled after great as Black writers such as Claude McKay, Nikki Giovanni as well as gospel and visual artists.

Finally, each trend chapter ends with a researcher's note poem using excerpts from my written and audio-recorded journals and observations. These final poems (in each section) invite readers inside my mind as I pondered my observations, reflections, and lingering questions. The purpose is to display the critical introspection and vulnerability need to reimagine education as an institution and classroom environments. This honest introspection is necessary for creating and sustaining a truth space indicates you are willingly surrendering your privilege and power to become a servant to others and help dismantle a racist and oppressive construct. Hooks (2012) contends "To return to love… we surrender the will to power… We cannot know love if we remain unable to surrender our attachment to power, if any feeling of vulnerability strikes terror in our hearts" (p. 221). I cannot ask for vulnerability if I am not willing to model this aspect for you. Each of these sections of the findings chapter and my analytic decisions made when creating them are discussed in the following sections.

Researcher's Note: A Preface

Chapter 5 begins with my introduction as a researcher. It reveals a novice researcher battling a myriad of emotions. I remember clearly the first day, my feelings becoming the foundation of the first researcher's note in Chapter 5. I arrived at the middle school early to allow time to set up the space. I eagerly parked in a space in the school's parking lot and grabbed my various bags. As my hand grasped the car door latch, I began to panic. I was not physically able to open my door. I stared in the rear-view mirror and realized I was breathing in short, quick, gasps. How could I stop this angst from coming forth? My ten-plus years as a middle school educator urged me that if I were not 100% real, the girls would sense the falsehoods. How could I ask them to be completely vulnerable if I was not willing to do so myself? To do so is sacrosanct to creating an environment of love and truth. I had to conquer my fear.

I closed my eyes and forced myself to slow down my breaths. I forced myself to inhale and count to three. One. Two. Three. I then exhaled slowly repeating the count. I repeated the process until both my breathing and pulse decreased. As I centered myself, a song danced through my mind. I exhaled once more, and began to softly sing, "Confession is good for the soul they say/well, now it's my turn/" (Robinson, 2000, Track 2). I realized at this moment, I needed to confess my fear. I furiously reached over to grab my researcher's journal and began to scribble words on the page. Before my eyes, the same phrase appeared over and over: Can I really do this? My eyes reread the repeated phrase and I realize I still was not calm, but sometimes as Maya Angelou (1970) wrote, "words mean more than what is set down on paper. It takes the human voice to infuse them with shades of deeper meaning" (p. 82). In short, I could not just write my confession, I felt that it must be spoken to have power. Deeper meaning could not be achieved by only professing the thoughts on paper; my spoken voice was necessary to add conviction and merit as well as cementing it as a form of knowledge and consciousness (Bell, 1992; Collins, 2000).

To infuse orality into my written words, I grabbed my cellphone and used its recording feature to confess what was on my soul; what was released was raw truth. I spoke in the language of my heart: poetry. The line ends were determined by the pauses I made as I gathered my thoughts. Although it was unplanned, the repetition of the lines, "Can I really do this?" provided cohesion and conveyed anxiousness and uncertainty. The poem, however, was not yet finalized. When I analyzed the transcriptions and replayed the audio recording, I realized gaps existed in my confession; places where a reader may be confused. Like Toni Morrison (1984), I wanted my writing to "urge the reader into active participation... which makes it difficult for the reader to confine himself to a cool and distant acceptance of data" (p. 387). To do so, required I clarify initial statements with specific examples derived from data and declarative words.

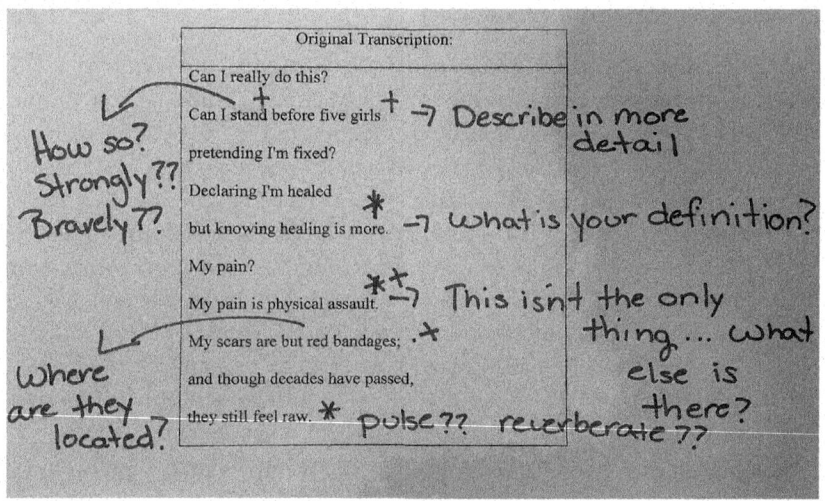

FIGURE 6.1 Text Annotation Revision Strategy

To revise the poem, I utilized a text annotation strategy (Beers & Probst, 2013) to discern areas which were to be strengthened. Text annotation involves marking a text by highlighting and adding words or notes. Text annotation requires close inspection of the text and allows the author to interact with memory and call to the present sights, sounds, and images which occurred in the moment. This strategy supported me in "bear [ing] witness and identify [ing] that which is useful from the past and that which ought to be discarded; it… ma [de] it possible to prepare for the present and live it out" (Morrison, 1984, p. 389). By annotating the poem, I desired to make the reader feel as if they were alongside me in the writing process. To annotate this poem, I highlighted in yellow the areas which required more details. I used other symbols to illustrate where I needed to add more details (+) or include more precise word choices (*) (Figure 6.1).

Introductions

Introducing my research partners and love advocates (Garnett, 2020), the Blue Diamond Girls, proved equally daunting. I wanted to capture them in their totality: all personality, energy, and life. Looking with eyes of love, I could easily view my research partners as authors and poets. Introducing the Blue Diamond girls required analyzing journal excerpts, excerpts from transcriptions as well as my field notes to produce descriptions which felt realistic and genuine to me (according to my interpretations) and the girls (as affirmed through member checking).

An important piece of data that supported the development of the introductory poems were the pictures I asked the girls to bring representing their personality. Around each picture, the girls wrote about what the image conveyed about their personality. Amir stood boldly in the image displaying the peace sign. Around her image, Amir wrote the words "Bold and Loud." Kelsey's image displayed her in the early morning donning a headscarf to protect her hair. She wears a confident yet knowing smile and she wrote the words, "Intelligent" beside her image. Melody's image displayed her shy nature indicates she utilized the phone to cover half of her face. Jennifer displayed her loquacious nature reveals her pictures included her surrounded by friends or family. Marie smiled widely in her image and her arms were wrapped around her body as if she were embracing herself. To the side of her picture, Marie wrote the words, "kind and loving." The descriptive words were interwoven in the introductory poems.

Another data source which supported the creation of introductions was the girl's journals. Each Blue Diamond girl was given a journal in which to capture their musings and share opinions which they may have wished to express aloud. The journal entries responded to the following prompt: If you really knew me, you would know? The responses could take place in any format they were comfortable with: bullets, pictures, sentences, or paragraphs. I wanted to ensure the Diamond Girls understood that it was not the medium but their voice and honesty that mattered. In this manner, the girls' voices, stories, and culture were used as a learning platform; they were a part of the community, and the community was essential for survival and growth (Johnson, Boutte, Greene, & Smith, 2018; Love, 2020; Muhammad, 2020; Waters, Evans-Winters, & Love, 2019). By using their journal responses and layering on notes regarding body language and personality traits from my research journal, the poems of introduction were born. Table 6.1 displays how I captured the newly formed characters from a variety of data points.

The composite introduction poems allow for the voices and personalities of the girls to be transparent while allowing the researcher to acknowledge ambiguities which occurred (Cook, 2013). This process of self-reflexivity makes analysis open for public consumption and allows for biases and assumptions to be revealed (Anfara, Brown, & Mangione, 2002). As this research is situated within Critical Race and Black Feminist paradigms, the constant reflections afforded me the opportunity to elucidate how my own "experiences, values, and positions… have influenced research interests, the way I choose to do their research and the ways I choose to represent their research findings" (Harrison, Macgibbon, & Morton, 2001, p. 325).

While the conception of the poems was fraught with emotion, they were easily born. In describing the development of the poems, I use the words "born" and "conception" decisively instead of "written" and "created" as they account

TABLE 6.1 Characterization Chart

Blue Diamond Girl	Selected Pseudonym	Journal Notes:	Researcher Notes
1	Amir	<ul><li>14 years old</li><li>Favorite Color: Green</li><li>Loud</li><li>Crazy</li><li>Love my Best Friend (Melody)</li><li>Love braids and cornrows</li></ul>	Observations: Amir's voice is usually the first you hear. She goes back and forth between confidant and insecure. She revealed she does not like her body since she feels she is too skinny. She often makes comments about hating having dark skin.
2	Melody	<ul><li>13 years old</li><li>Favorite Color: Pink</li><li>Shy</li><li>Quiet</li><li>3 Siblings</li></ul>	Observations: Incredibly quiet and introverted. Melody does not like speaking in groups. She revealed she does not talk much in school at all, though she often smiles She admits she has some issues with her body.
3	Kelsey	<ul><li>14 years old</li><li>Favorite Color: Blue</li><li>3 Siblings</li><li>Intelligent</li><li>I know everybody.</li><li>Love clothes & fashion</li></ul>	Observations: Prides herself on being in advanced classes. Switches from African American Language to Mainstream English. She revealed loving her body as it is but wishes she could make her gut a little smaller. Quite confidant and boasts about how boys find her attractive.
4	Jennifer	<ul><li>13 years old</li><li>Favorite Colors: Black, Blue</li><li>Talkative</li><li>Older sister; younger brother</li><li>Hobbies: Talking, Phone, Movies</li></ul>	Observations: Jennifer is one of the first persons to join a conversation. She is the middle child and loves to talk, talk, and talk. She often discusses how she cannot wait until she is older. She revealed she has a hard time gaining weight despite the fact she is constantly eating.
5	Marie	<ul><li>13 years old</li><li>Favorite Color: Red</li><li>Rude</li><li>I tell people about themselves quickly.</li><li>I have anger issues.</li><li>Funny</li><li>Intelligent</li><li>Kind (Somewhat)</li></ul>	Observations: Marie is willing to "read" anyone and tell them about themselves. She often comes into the meetings upset but the anger dissolves quickly. Marie gives me a hug before leaving every meeting. The only caveat is that she waits until everyone leaves so no one will know about it.

for the interplay of emotions, creativity, ideas, sounds, and words. This writing process was time-consuming and painful, traversing euphoria and rage. This rage is not new. It is an emotion for resistance and resilience and has been commonplace for Blacks throughout time and history. James Baldwin (1961) was asked about being Black in America and he responded:

> To be a Negro in this country and to be relatively conscious is to be in a state of rage almost, almost all of the time — and in one's work. And part of the rage is this: It isn't only what is happening to you. But it's what's happening all around you and all of the time in the face of the most extraordinary and criminal indifference, indifference of most white people in this country, and their ignorance. Now, since this is so, it is a great temptation to simplify the issues under the illusion that if you simplify them enough, people will recognize them. I think this illusion is very dangerous because, in fact, it isn't the way it works. A complex thing can't be made simple. You simply have to try to deal with it in all its complexity and hope to get that complexity across.
>
> (p. 205)

As educators, we cannot seek to simplify racism's destruction. We must bravely dare to discuss its complex nuances. The ultimate creation, the introduction poem, is carefully crafted, thought-out, planned, and a result of endless reading and rereading of data. The remaining poems build on the introductions, serving not only as a method of representing carefully analyzed data but as both anchor and life-raft, helping me share interpretations of the girls' truths and to display how much work still needs to be done for traditional classrooms to become liberative spaces. In the process, as a member as well as the researcher within our truth space, I began to make peace with my difficult history.

Fat

It is no secret; girls in close social circles discuss body dissatisfaction, expound on weight-loss strategies, and/or commiserate over an inability to lose weight (Cox, 2020; Taylor, 2018). Despite this fact, body image is difficult to discuss in educational settings as it is often painful and controversial. For example, Nichter (2000) conducted an ethnographic study of middle school girls engaging in fat talk and found some girls believed maintaining silence in a group of girls expressing body dissatisfaction would imply they considered themselves and their bodies to be above reproach. This is why the findings from our truth space are so vital to academic pursuit and educational transformation as they center research on the Black girls' struggle with obtaining actualization and utilize a social context and lived realities as a critical backdrop to discuss weight, body image, and race (Beauboeuf-Lafontant, 2003).

Fat: A Poem of Definition

This poem opens this dissertation's data-driven representations of The Blue Diamond Girls' conceptions of *fat* by providing contextualization on how fat is perceived by many different society members. For example, represented in the poem is the American Medical Association and Center for Disease Control views, both describing obesity as a serious public health crisis impacting 35% of adults in the United States (Overweight and Obesity Statistics, 2012). In addition, mass media depicts television shows in which obese individuals are stereotyped or ridiculed as well as centering dialogues on individual-level causes of obesity and omitting the societal, economic, and environmental contributors (Cox, 2020; Taylor, 2018). Alongside these perspectives, are the belief systems and values we adopt from family and friends. To determine how messages regarding obesity were conveyed in families, interviews were used. The interviews asked each Blue Diamond girl to reflect upon memories and experiences in which they learned values and beliefs around food, body size, and weight. In one story, Melody recalled waiting for hours with her mother in the gym as she exercised trying to lose the dreaded baby weight. Marie described her grandmother's surefire strategy for losing weight: Closing your mouth. Kelsey described incidents of being teased in the hallway regarding her body size. These are the contextual forces problematizing the issue of obesity and shaping the ideas, assumptions, and beliefs of the research partners.

Fat: A Visual Poem

The poem *Fat: A Visual Poem* was created through an analysis of the Blue Diamonds' thoughts on obesity. One way I solicited those thoughts was by employing two different book club activities. For the first activity, I wanted the girls to provide responses to three words which are pervasive in obesity discourse: skinny, thick, and fat/obese. The words were placed in their journals and each girl was given time to individually respond to the words. These words serve as powerful descriptors and build upon one another to create a political force which "works [s] to incite, reinforce, control, monitor, optimize, and organize the forces under it" (Foucault, 1978, p. 136). I wanted to better understand the ways in which differences – particularly those which exist on an inherent binary system such as thin/thick, skinny/fat – are constructed and maintained. This enabled me to better discern how the girls construct reality through language and cultural practices (Gordon, Council, Dukes, & Muhammad, 2019). Table 6.2 captures the individual responses.

The second activity asked the girls to respond to visual representations of the words: skinny, thick, fat, and obese. The images were selected by using a Google Boolean word search. Having responses to both words and visual images reinforces the notion of literacy being a fluid multimodal process including linguistic,

TABLE 6.2 Word Association Responses

Club Member	Skinny	Thick	Fat/Obese
Amir	• Pretty • Don't weigh much • Light-skinned • Don't like to eat	• Dark-Skinned • Big Butt • Gets attention	• Ugly • Fat face • Loves to eat • Loves Little Debbie • Can't walk
Melody	• Perfect • Smaller clothes • 80–90 lbs. • Can find anything in their size • More beautiful	• Not as big • Bigger clothes • Little Stomach • Can barely walk • Fat Hands	• Bigger Sizes • Can't do some things because of their size • Some parts of their body may be skinny • Stomach touches the steering wheel when driving • No Neck • Fat Feet • Can't fit into chairs • Stomach hanging out
Kelsey	• Bones • No Butt	• Nice Shape	• Uncomfortable • Embarrassing
Jennifer	• Perfect • In shape • Light-Weight • Never eats • No Booty • Can barely fit clothes • Gets Boys • Always wears make-up	• Booty • Can dress • Gets attention • Eats but not too much • Inner thighs touch together • More Hair	• Don't care about themselves • Double Chin • No clothes • Rolls on neck • Eats • Can fit into clothes • Can't sit up • Tries to be skinny • Tries to fit into skinny people clothes • Never shaves
Marie	• Boney • No meat • Cute but boney	• Identifies herself as this • Pretty • Thick everything includes thighs, butt, etc.	• Needs help to stop eating • Very big • Ugly • Have more than three stomach rolls • Humongous • Does not exercise

visual, audio, and spatial elements each in constant interplay to form the foundation of communication (Gonzalez & González Ybarra, 2020). By accepting sociocultural literacy learning, educators recognize and legitimize the deep funds of knowledge (González, Moll, & Amanti, 2009) that students bring from home. This theory rejects deficit-based learning and insists on building on students' inherent strength. By asking them to analyze both linguistic and visual texts, the Blue Diamond Girls "read the world and the word" (Freire & Macedo, 1987) which helped me verify particular data points. Table 6.3 illustrates individual responses.

TABLE 6.3 Visual Image Responses

	Skinny	*Thick*	*Fat/Obese*
Amir	• Gets lots of boys • Model • Party Girl • Pretty • Works out	• Loves' to eat • Doesn't work out • Doesn't have friends • Fat	• Doesn't work out • Obese • Loves to eat • No friends • NOT a model • Tough Life
Melody	• She doesn't eat • Model • Her life in school is easy • Lots of Friends	• Eats a lot but not that much • Thick girl • Life in school is hard • Gets teased	• Poor • Life is very hard • Gets picked on • Obese • Eats junk food all day
Kelsey	• She likes to show her curves • Boys want her • Fast • Hangs with boys	• Party Girl • Thick • Boys like her • Expresses her culture	• That girl big! • People pick at her and call her names • At home eating her feelings • Eats a lot
Jennifer	• Model • Popular • Doesn't eat anything	• Big one • Confident • Eats and likes to do nothing • Doesn't work out	• Obese • She is too big to sit in chairs • Gets picked on • Lives in a dirty neighborhood • Eats and sleeps a lot
Marie	• Model • Bold • Will probably end up pregnant • Fast • Exercises	• College girl • Wants to find a man • Spoiled • thick	• Obese • Doesn't work out • Fat • Lives at home with cats

It was quite clear; the girls internalized a mechanistic view of the body which focuses on an assumed relationship between obesity, inactivity, poor dieting, and major health issues (Cox, 2020; Oliver, 2006; Taylor, 2018). No comment more clearly elucidates this idea than Amir's comments proclaiming the girl labeled fat/obese could not be a fashion model and must have experienced a difficult life. Analyzing the data, revealed a reality in which the fat/obese individual's body is perceived as being a lazy body which should be disciplined and submitted to scrutiny and investigation (Murray, 2007, 2008). The challenge was how to convey the mass of emotional responses in poetic form. The answer came after reviewing a transcription in which the girls discussed the fat/obese image, in which the girls responded in the following manner:

KELSEY: It seems like every ten minutes or so I saw his fat behind eating. I told him he needed to stop that. Fat people is obese.
AMIR: What about their big legs? They jiggle. Jiggle. Jiggle.
JENNIFER: No clothes. They can't wear clothes like they wear a shower curtain for clothes.
MELODY: Overweight. When they sit down, they can't get up. People have to help them.
MARIE: They got a double-chin. Rolls upon rolls. What's that show called? "My 600 LB Life" on TLC! I was watching that the other day and I was laughing. It ain't hard to lose weight… all they gotta do is stop shoveling food in their mouths.

As I listened to their voices and reread their descriptions, an image began to appear in my mind: a grainy black and white photograph portraying an obese individual with the prerequisite "rolls upon rolls of fat." This would be a new form: visual poetry. A form which combined multiple modalities and as such modifies the relationship between printed word and image. Changing the text's materiality unavoidably changes the way we read/receive the text" (Kress, 2003). I utilized Tagxedo, a website which allows a user to blend words and visual images; the visual poem needed dual modalities to convey its truth. The image, however, would display the words used to describe fat/obese. This image seemed apropos as it represented the literal weight of the fat and the symbolic traumatic burden of teasing, ridicule, and being a constant spectacle. The individual needed to be isolated to reflect the notion of being lonely but also to symbolize the reoccurring message that obesity's cause and solution reside within the individual. A notion echoed by Marie, stating, "It ain't hard to lose weight… stop shoveling food." The pervasiveness of the personal reasonability myth plays a major role in obesity stigma and serves to justify stigmatization as an acceptable societal response (Schott, 2016). I hoped the reader would find the picture halting and difficult to process, therefore causing a pause to take in both its form and content. Since form mediates understanding (Eisner, 1991) using the visual poem as a non-traditional text, brings new and unexpected insights into the world of an often-overlooked experience: that of the fat/obese individual.

FAT: A Biography in Five Short Chapters

This series of poems was modeled after Portia Nelson's (1989) *Autobiography in Five Short Chapters*. The poem cleverly uses the metaphor of a narrator attempting to avoid falling into a hole to discuss overcoming an obstacle. Although poignant, the poem cleverly uses five succinct stanzas, each having only 30–40 words. Reproducing the style and power of this poem posed the challenge of minimalism, yet it was the minimalistic structure which posed a solution. The poem was reminiscent of a genre popularized by youth culture which emphasizes authenticity and brevity in 140 characters or less: the meme. Coined by Richard Dawkins (1976), memes are a cultural phenomenon usually involving jokes, quirky wisdom, and pictures which "which subtly represents the tones of today's social etiquette and culture.... The cultural impact of Memes cannot be ignored. In fact, it can even be a tool for self-promotion, branding, and marketing" (Hines & Cass, 2011, p. 1). In short, the meme represents a cultural artifact divulging insight into a particular event.

It was the idea of branding which percolated through my mind as I pondered how the Blue Diamond Girls would brand fat. I challenged the girls to think of the day and life of fat and asked: If fat were personified and could speak, what it would say? Figure 6.2 explains the meme activity.

After, reading the instructions, Jennifer proclaimed, "Chile, that ain't hard," and the girls settled down at computers to compose their creations. As they scrolled through Google searching for images, the room was littered with vocal outbursts and laughter. Screens filled with pictures of scales screaming "help" and obese individuals in depraved acts of indulgence. Each time, the images were never challenged or questioned, just accepted as an unmitigated truth. Within 20 minutes, the creations were unveiled. As co-author, I only had to arrange them in a manner which conveyed a cohesive structure with a beginning, middle, and end.

Stereotypes

Analyzing the memes proved insightful into the girls' thoughts. As texts, memes examine how "multimodal literacy practices with online popular culture are changing conceptions of texts and of rhetorical concepts such as audience and authorship; the ways in which issues of politics, power, and resistance influence such literacy practices" (Williams & Zenger, 2012, p. x). Interpreting the memes unearthed perceptions not conveyed through traditional communicative discourse. An overarching pattern I constructed was the overwhelming abundance of stereotypical ideals held by The Blue Diamond Girls such as constantly

FIGURE 6.2 Meme Activity

indulging in oversized portions of unhealthy foods or the tendency to be and remain inert. Table 6.4 displays the meme analysis.

Experts argue that since the transition from childhood to adolescence is marked by increased attention to beauty ideals (Taylor, 2018) and there exists longevity in memory for weight-related media messages (Cox, 2020), there is a relational aggression toward obese peers (Janssen, Craig, Boyce, & Pickett, 2004). For this reason, the stereotypes needed to be explored in more detail. They were worthy of a poem all their own; a poem which distorted font size and white space to symbolize the distorted perceptions of obesity. The words from the poem were derived as the Blue Diamond girls did a gallery walk of the memes. This allowed time for girls to interrogate the images.

TABLE 6.4 Meme Analysis

Meme Pattern	Researcher Analysis
Describing Fat	• All the memes feature someone who would be characterized as being morbidly obese. • All the memes feature individuals who are sitting or lying down. This indicates the girls see an obese individual as being someone who is inactive and does not exercise. • The theme of "not fitting" reoccurs throughout the memes. Either the individual does not fit into their clothing (Meme 5), or not being able to fit into a chair (Meme 2). • 3/5 memes feature someone eating. The girls could possibly see this as a characteristic of obesity. In the pictures featuring food, the food is also oversized. This could be an indication of excessive eating habits as well. It also reinforces the notion of the obese individual always being hungry as indicated in Meme 3. • Another reoccurring pattern is the theme of being out of control and needing assistance. Meme 1 features an individual in need of assistance as if their weight is so out of control an outside force is needed to intervene. • In all of the memes, the individual is alone, typically with food. • None of them pictures a fashionable individual.

Stereotypes	• Always eating
	   o Insatiable hunger
	   o Over-sized portions
	• Not exercising
	   o Lazy
	   o In need of an outside force to exhibit control
	• Not fashionable
	   o Clothes which do not fit properly
	• No control
	   o (See above)

Stigma	• The girls often laughed and pointed as they designed the memes as if obesity is a site of humor or an exhibited. • The image of the scale with the words "Help me," once again reinforces the notion of being out of control. Even more so, Amir tried to put this label on Melody, as an insult. • The images reinforce the notion of isolation with food as the only consolation • In one image, the girls were laughing so hard they failed to notice an error in the meme. The individual is eating a hotdog, but it is labeled as a hamburger. When I pointed this out, Kelsey declared, "It's still funny."

As the girls conducted their meme gallery walk, carefully studying the images created by each other, Melody softly inquired of the group, "You really think all fat people do is eat?" Amir replied, "I eat all the time and I can't gain weight." Marie pushed the idea even further, "So, why do they gain weight?" There was something affirming about our truth space as words could be left open to the wind, and there they would exist with less judgment. It was not a fundamental mind shift. In fact, only a few questions were uttered; yet, it was still an opportunity of change and as a fat woman with concerns about the field of education and students experiencing size, race, and gender oppression, I felt hopeful. This activity provided credence for the need to incorporate new literacies, such as memes, as they create new opportunities to interpret our world.

Fat: A Confessional Spoken-Word Performance Poem

This poem was built from data that illuminated our truth space as a confessional; a space to ask questions, share stories, and feel free. We were but "strangers learning to worship the strangers around" us (Jordan, 1977). There was no putting on fo' company here. Oftentimes while we worked, braids would be done or undone as needed. Food would be passed around the table and enjoyed by all. The girls would remove their shoes and sit with bare feet or in colorful socks. We spoke our home tongue, the African American Language, and feared no reprisals. I heard stories of family members in prison and the darkness of depression. I shared my fears on battling grief. Received and administered hugs as medicine. Honesty came in one style: brutal and it was never revoked, always welcomed. We were a safety net and a structure resembling a family in construction and purpose. Townsend, Thomas, & Jackson-Lowman (2013) discuss the role of this kind of community as embraced and influenced by "othermothers" and sister circles as a critical support system in the socialization process of African American girls. Othermothers are the equivalent of mothers while sister circles are a space for women to come together as healing partners (Townsend, Thomas, & Jackson-Lowman, 2013). Othermothers and sister circles can be important vehicles for truth spaces as they provide critical lessons about confronting oppression with the younger generation. Data led me to believe that this was indeed our confessional.

For example, when I asked the girls to describe life as a fat adolescent, I patiently awaited their honesty. The responses were succinct but raw:

MARIE: Very tough!
KELSEY: Hard!
AMIR: Yeah....it ain't easy!
MELODY: Embarrassing.
JENNIFER: It's very hard.
ME: Why?

MELODY: Because they get bullied, laughed at, name-calling... They called "fatty," "ugly" and "stank."
MARIE: Everything but they name.

As I probed further for details, the memories quickly unfolded. Examples ranged from overweight students being pushed on the stairwells or teased and mocked as they walked down the hallways. The cafeteria became an event in and of itself as they recounted students collecting cookies to eat or bargaining for additional portions. The analysis of these data led to the representation of these stories in the performance poem. It needed to be displayed in such a way to pay homage to the exuberant personalities and the sanctity of the club space. Spoken-word poetry seemed the perfect solution as it affirmed Black culture by using storytelling, call and response, home languages, and oral tradition (Baker-Bell, 2020; Boutte, 2015; Johnson et al., 2018). It also has the potential to bond the poet with the audience opening the way for passionate expressions and ethical insights (Weiss & Herndon, 2001). This poem was testimony, social commentary, and a call to action. It was *literocracy*: the amalgamation of literacy, democracy, and action (Fisher, 2005; Kinloch, 2005) and seemed a perfect way to conclude the section on fat.

Researcher's Note: The Skinny on Fat

The researcher's note on fat reflects my interpretation of the turmoil of all research partners. As I watched the Blue Diamond girls discuss the complexity of obesity, they shifted between stances: internalized hatred or unapologetic resistance. I did not want to overlook this flux in my representation of findings as it affirms a simple truth: As an American society, we are confounded by obesity. Fat ushers in a realm of emotions including pity, hatred, envy, and at the most compassionate of times, love. The discussions elicited more questions for further study, but it cemented the need for a truth space to discuss issues. This thought permeated my mind as it dominants not only in society, but also in the data, and I wanted it to stay with the reader. Therefore, I made it the last lines of the poem. If the reader walked away with nothing else, I wanted this idea to remain.

Colorism

Blue-Black. Red-Bone. Mulatto. High Yella – These are all words and phrases I scarcely thought the Blue Diamond Girls would recognize even less say. Yet, the words were uttered daily. Colorism or discrimination based on skin tone is a persistent problem for people of Color in the United States and around the world (Russell-Cole, Wilson, & Hall, 2013; Woodson, 2020). For African American girls, colorism may manifest as a preference for physical characteristics they believe will be judged more favorably such as lighter skin and smoother hair. This skin color hierarchy privileges light-skinned people of Color over dark-skinned in areas such as income, education, housing, beauty, and marriage and is "directly related to the larger system of racism in the USA and around the world. The color complex is also exported around the globe, in part through America's media images, and helps to sustain the multibillion-dollar skin bleaching and cosmetic surgery industries" (Hunter, 2007, p. 237). It is the persistent tension with melanin having emotional and psychological ramifications as individuals, in particular, adolescent girls, shift between reveling in and rebuking their skin tone (Jacobs, 2016). The poem "*Colorism: A Definition Poem*" built upon this shift.

Colorism: A Definition Poem

Due to the strong influence of the majority's standard of beauty and African American's minority status, it is widely believed that adopting and internalizing Western beauty standards is advantageous. A study which examined skin color in the lives of 123 African American adolescents (aged 11–19 years) found complexion to be related to self-esteem, but the study also brought additional complexity to the issue. Students who self-reported as "lighter" or "darker" had lower levels of satisfaction with their skin color than did students whose skin color was classified as "somewhere in between" (Woodson, 2020). As an issue impacting the Black community, colorism has been tackled by both CRT and Black Feminist scholars who have identified colorism as a cause of internal differentiation and inequality (Bonilla-Silva & Ray, 2008; Hooks, 1992). Delgado (2000) argued that colorism is yet another example of binary thinking which "exceptionalizes and thus obscures other experiences" and "pits minority groups against each other" (p. 75). If left unchecked, this internalized oppression can lead to self-hatred, dangerous behaviors such as higher sexual risk, and increased substance abuse (Townsend, Thomas, & Jackson-Lowman, 2013).

I wanted these ideals to be conveyed in the poem of definition. I carefully scoured research on colorism to determine which phrases and sentences portrayed these ideals the best and include these items in the poem. Although apt descriptions, I felt something was missing. For the final line of the poem, I reflect on my personal experience and thought how best I could describe the turmoil of wanting to bleach my skin. The words "emotional terrorism" appeared in my mind and I quickly scribbled them on the page as they seemed fit to describe the internal warfare which can block self-actualization.

The Color Complex: An Introduction

For me as a researcher, the issue of colorism is more personal than statistics in a journal. Thus, my journal reflections and data from the girls' activities and conversations were analyzed together leading to the creation of *The Color Complex*. The importance of this poem was vivid throughout the data but particularly

FIGURE 6.3 Skin Tone Scale

illuminated one day when, while waiting on the arrival of the girls for a book club, I received a call from Amir's teacher who was deeply concerned. She had overheard Amir in the hallway confessing her desire for blue eyes and beauty. As I listened, I was immediately struck by the parallels to Morrison's protagonist in *The Bluest Eye* (1994) and I did not want Amir to suffer Pecola's fate. This was an issue that could not be silenced since to do so in the face of such bold assaults would be to aid in complicity (Hooks, 1995). To enact change, we needed to use our truth space to delve into the complexities of skin color.

Further data reflected in this poem came from our activity analyzing skin tone bias. I introduced the Black Doll/white Doll Test in which Kenneth and Mamie Clarke (1946) utilized dolls to determine Black and white children's racial preference and concluded the children had internalized society's racist messages, often choosing the white dolls as the as the most desirable and often ascribed positive characteristics to it. The Clarkes concluded segregation produced a feeling of inferiority in African American children. Since 1946, many researchers have revisited this critical study. Bergen (2009) wrote about how Black children suffered from wounded self-esteem as a result. Instead of dolls, I asked the Blue Diamond girls to analyze a skin tone scale (Figure 6.3) to note which skin tone, if any, they found the most beautiful, and which skin tone, if any, they found the least attractive.

The girls circled their preferences, reflected on the decisions in their journals, and discussed their choices as a whole group. Their discussions were quite revealing as displayed in this transcript excerpt:

AMIR: I picked the dark skin as the least attractive because you know dark skin… the real dark skin people have big lips and they don't look right with big lips. People say I got big lips and I look good with my big lips, but I'm not real dark skin.

KELSEY: (*Describing the least attractive*) The person was too dark with pretty skin tone. The skin tone that was the most attractive was the light skin tone because it was beautiful, and I just loved it.

MELODY: The pretty one is not too dark and not too light. I chose that one because it is pretty, and it is the most attractive.

MARIE: The least attractive is the darkest one and I chose that one because it's too dark.

JENNIFER: The too Black skin tone is too dark, and no one can see you if you are too dark. Someone will call you African or say you are from Haiti. You are perfect if you are light skin because you are light and bright. That skin tone gets more attention and more boys.

As I listened to their explanations, my heart hurt. It was as Bishop (2007) stated:

> Racism by its very nature is so insidious that some Black people have internalized negative attitudes, left over from the days of slavery, toward themselves and their appearance. Thus, lighter skin color and straight hair have often been more highly valued even among Black people than darker skin and kinky hair.
>
> (p. 231)

Once again, my poetic muse and I were challenged with how to present this truth. I looked at the Blue Diamond's transcripts and was confused on how to synthesize meaning from their musings. I realized that I needed a theory to guide me and reached for my copy of *The Color Complex: The Politics of Skin Color among African Americans* (Russell-Cole et al., 2013). As I sat down and began to read the introduction, I was struck with inspiration. The words on the page seemed to change. Some words appeared more pronounced while others faded into the background; I was staring into another aspect of visual poetry: The Blackout Poem (Kleon, 2010).

Blackout poetry focuses on rearranging words to create a different meaning. Also known as newspaper blackout poetry, the author uses a permanent marker to remove whatever words or images are deemed unnecessary or irrelevant. The principal idea is to formulate a completely new text from previously recognized words and images, which the reader is free to interpret. Blackout Poetry is advantageous as it challenges both authors and readers to confront "a different way of seeing the words on the paper and thus a different way of thinking about what those words communicate and why they matter. Like critical thinking, blackout poetry is a process of revelation, an uncovering of meaning (Ladenheim, 2014). The poem was inside the text and only had to be revealed. Like a word carver, I chipped away at the text. I moved from transcript to opening pages of *The Color Complex* circling the emotions and ideas which coincided with the emotions and ideas located in the opening pages: the guilt, anger, and embarrassment which lay just beneath the skin. I grabbed my pen and blacked-out words until the final piece was completed.

Dark Girls: A Poem in Two Voices

In Channsin-Berry & Duke, 2011, Bill Duke and D. Channsin Berry released the documentary *Dark Girls* which focused on celebrating the beauty of melanin. The directors wanted to counteract the emotional and psychological attacks which Black girls who have darker skin, face daily. It was to serve as the point of reflection to "counter [our] realities of violence and discrimination by envisioning the Black female community as a collective of unique agents working toward a common goal of liberation" (Blackmon, 2009, p. 3). This liberative stance can only be achieved through critical discussions which analyze critique and challenge the Eurocentric ideal that "white is the only right." The Blue Diamond's conversations on skin tone afforded instructional conversations on resisting stereotypical images. The conversations did not always take place whole group, sometimes learning occurred between friends. Amir and Kelsey often debated the perception of darker skin and beauty ideals.

Amir did not find her skin to be beautiful. This was revealed through comments in the book club, her journal, and through discussion surrounding the skin tone activity when she selected her own skin tone, the darker one, as the least attractive. In the same data, I understood Kelsey to embrace her dark skin and boldly declare her beauty. Thus, the poem *Dark Girls* is a composite poem created by selecting data excerpts representing analyses of journals entries and discussions. Reflecting Kelsey and Amir, it is a poem for two voices (Fleischman & Beddows, 1988) composed to be read aloud by two readers. Most lines in these poems are spoken by the individual reader separately, and the speakers take turns going back and forth between the voices; however, some lines are composed to be spoken at the same time by both speakers.

This poetic genre has several benefits including its creative way of displaying dueling perspectives, in this case, from the discussion on what defines beauty. The format is reminiscent of being in a conversation and is both familiar and attractive. In the poem, Kelsey's voice was a message of love and healing helping to guide Amir through her negative internalizations.

Heart's Desire: Colorism in Action

This was by far one of the easiest poems to birth; although it involved intense study as I revisited the transcripts several times. The lines were comprised by layering different lines from a skin tone discussion after carefully analyzing those data juxtaposed with other data from our truth space. This process was time-consuming yet rewarding as it provided opportunities for triangulation. The girls all discussed why many of them found light-skinned guys more desirable. The conversation unfolded as follows:

KELSEY: I really think that a light-skinned boy is the best.
JASMINE: Why?
AMIR: They act right. They act better.
MARIE: No, don't even say that.
AMIR: It is! A light-skinned guy makes pretty babies.
KELSEY: My boo ain't light.
MELODY: (Laughing) You have kids with him your kids ain't gonna be right.
KELSEY: I know this boy he mixed with Caucasian. He mixed with Puerto-Rican and Black. He got gray eyes. He is… whoa!
MARIE: Light-skinned boys lick their lips and it is just sexy. When a dark-skinned boy does it, it is just like, "What are you doin' son?"
JENNIFER: I ain't ever seen a light-skinned boy that didn't look good.
KELSEY: Like Ellison (*pseudonym*) 'Member when he got here? His face was perfect. His hair was slicked down and walked up into the cafeteria liked he owned it.
AMIR: I want my baby to have blue eyes. They say if you marry a white man, then your baby's eyes will be blue.

In Amir's mind, for her child to be beautiful, she or he needed to have lighter skin and blue eyes. Therefore accepting the Western beauty aesthetic as the ultimate form is dangerous as it stands in direct opposition to the Black body. As Collins (2000) pointed out, the Black body becomes the "Other" as "[b]lue-eyed, blond, thin women could not be considered beautiful without the Other – Black women with classical African features of dark skin, broad noses, full lips, and kinky hair" (p. 79). The process of "othering" which Collins beautifully describes could not occur without the Black girls/women's bodies being hijacked and utilized for white supremacy's hateful purposes; in this case, it is to uphold white beauty ideals while devaluing Black beauty. It was this very conflict, which prompted the discussion in the poem Dark Girls. If also, we consider that property and wealth are things that can be passed from generation to generation, then too, we must consider Amir's legacy to her child.

Let me be clear, I fully understand that when CRT was created, the tenet of whiteness as property referred to ownership and property rights. I argue here, however, that this principle should be expanded to include other aspects of ownership such as laying claim to the Black body. Harris (1993) contends that:

> whiteness shares the critical characteristics of property even as the meaning of property has changed over time. In particular, whiteness and property share a common premise – a conceptual nucleus – of a right to exclude. This conceptual nucleus has proven to be a powerful center around which

whiteness as property has taken shape. Following the period of slavery and conquest, white identity became the basis of racialized privilege that was ratified and legitimated in law as a type of status property. After legalized segregation was overturned, whiteness as property evolved into a more modern form through the law's ratification of the settled expectations of relative white privilege as a legitimate and natural baseline.

(p. 1714)

Amir felt the pull of being an "other" and felt that it could not be redeemed within her lifetime. Instead, she wanted her progeny to achieve an ideal she would never obtain. It was not enough to be light-skinned. For Amir, her child must be deeply saturated with whiteness – a level which can only be accomplished through marrying a white man and bearing a child with beautiful blue eyes. Amir's desire displays a need to cleanse her Black body and its supposed ugliness with that of whiteness. This painful self-flagellation is part of the legacy she will extend to her daughter. I wanted the reader to be haunted by Amir's declaration. To achieve this, that confession needed a visual distance. I wanted the last 12 words to appear as if they are falling away from the poem as a tear would fall away from the eye.

Researcher's Note: Delving into Skin

Colorism is not a new concept. Its roots extend back to European colonialism (Jordan, 1986) and the plantation system of enslaved African Americans. Slavery was a brutal form of white domination which rewarded those who emulated whiteness culturally, ideologically, economically, and aesthetically (Hunter, 2007). In the poem, I wanted to recognize Colorism roots by connecting it to familial roots. I wanted to parallel my issues with Colorism with the tensions and issues of my research partners. Decades may have passed, but the power and allure of color subjugation still permeated both our realities.

Intersectionality

Picture a woman standing before you. She is simultaneously whole and yet fragmented. From a glance, her race, size, and gender may be discerned. She stands as a proud Black woman blessed to see 43 years of age. Yet, it is not as easy to discern her career, sexual orientation, or religious/spiritual beliefs. She is fragmented yet whole. In a court of law, she is seen as either Black or a woman, but rarely ever does the legal system consider the complementing social identities at the same time. This can be seen when analyzing the racially and gendered biased tensions of Black women wearing braids in the workforce (Ainsworth, 2013) or the sentencing of Black women in criminal cases (Gatewood & Norris, 2019; Morris, 2016). The fragmenting of identity in the legal realm is the center of the intersectionality critique. Our truth space further builds on this fragmentation by adding the additional layer of body size and how it affects perceptions and treatment.

Coined by legal scholar Kimberle' Crenshaw (1989), the notion of intersectionality regarding race emerged from CRT and analyzes "the multidimensionality of marginalized subjects' lived experiences" (p. 139) noting that identity cannot only be analyzed by examining the identity fragments but must include a close examination of the combined totality of lived experiences. The central principles of the intersectionality of race and gender have long research lineage and have also been embraced by Black Feminists (Beale, 1971; Collins, 1998). This fundamental tenant undergirds the following section of poems.

Intersectionality: A Definition Poem

Intersectionality: A Definition Poem was created to provide the reader background on the complexity and significance of exploring the combination of social identities. One of the most important aspects of this poem was the attention to broad tenets which comprise intersectionality. First, it critiques the race/gender binaries most often used in identity politics; lived realities are dynamic forces and are heavily influenced by different social factors impacting one another. Second, it provides a vocabulary to challenge dominant ideology. When analyzing social issues, one cannot predetermine which social identity is the most important; it must be contextualized within the moment. Finally, intersectionality provides a framework for recognizing and acknowledging exclusionary practices used to analyze lived experiences of Black women. Black Feminist Theory argues analyzing oppressive constructs must simultaneously occur over several levels (Collins, 2000; Nash, 2013). This linking allows reveals a stronger connection between individual experiences to broader institutional structures such as health care, education, and finances. Ultimately, intersectionality is geared toward social transformation. By undertaking this multi-level analysis, subtle power structures can be exposed and changed (Hankivsky, 2014). Intersectionality is also essential to analyzing the turmoil of the Blue Diamond girls navigating adolescence within an educational power structure and was selected as a key section in the findings.

Bearing Witness: Life as a Black Girl

This poem is Jennifer's. I present it not as a composite of data but as Jennifer's words standing alone. I only added the introduction and conclusion and made choices about how many words to place on each line but the words are hers as spoken during one of our group meetings when I asked the girls to respond to the following question in their journals: What is it like being a Black girl at

Houston Middle School? The girls journaled over the weekend and we were to discuss their responses the following Tuesday. Their responses were as follows:

KELSEY: I wanna go! (She begins to read her journal topic.) How is it like being a Black girl in Houston? It's bad because we can't wear short stuff. We can't get away with things that white people get away with… Can't even have out our phones like the other kids. I'm thick and pretty and people hate on me and wish they could be me. I feel like we (students) are being segregated like they were back in the day because we are not treated right same as it was back then.

MELODY: It's a lot of drama about everybody wanting to fight. It is a lot of drama about everybody wanting to fight. Some of them just don't know how to act. They either just don't like them, or they just want to cause something between them.

AMIR: It's like slavery because they treat Black people differently from white people. The white people get to wear anything they want but when Black people wear shorts, we have to call our parents to bring us other stuff. But life here is bad for Black people.

MARIE: It's just kind of difficult. Most of the white teachers think that you are not that bright about what you say or do. So, they think that automatically you are going to make wrong choices or the mistakes.

JENNIFER: (Reading from her journal.) I think it is difficult because of how the way white kids they look… (She stops reading and just begins to talk.) They look at Black kids and judge them on how smart they are, and some teachers think… If you are the only Black kid in the class then you are the slow person. I think that… um… when most white people see Black students, they automatically think they were raised in the "hood." Which is not sometimes true but most of it is not.

All the responses depicted being Black as being treated differently in shape or form whether it be with clothing, enforcing rules, or the use of technology. The responses all shed light on the use of a deficit-based perspective (Boutte, 2015; Gay, 2010) in classroom instruction where they were aware of a presupposition that Black students do not have the necessary skills to master grade-level skills. The girls also indicated observing or receiving harsher punishment for rule enforcement which we know to be a major contributor to the school to prison pipeline (Morris, 2016, 2019; Schott Foundation for Public Education, 2016). Sadly, their responses also revealed internalized racism where the girls accepted and believed stereotypes about their racial group including increased fights and prevalence of drama (Kohli, Johnson, & Perez, 2006). As these were dominant views across data sources and both CRT and Black Feminist Theory argue that until these topics are named and discussed within schools, we inhibit our move toward racial and social justice, these were important elements to illuminate in this findings poem.

Jennifer was eager to provide an example of the daily discrimination faced by Black girls at Houston Middle. The other Blue Diamond Girls and I sat with rapt attention as she told her story of "The Tale of Two Girls." The tale recounts her experiences in poetic structure. As co-author, I only felt the need to add the introductory and concluding stanzas for cohesion. These too, however, were based on Jennifer's words since, when I asked her to provide more detail about life as a Black girl, she looked at me and said, "You really want to know this? Cause you ain't gonna like it." This shockingly honest response seemed the perfect introduction and conclusion to her tale and elucidates why "race and class can never be just 'subtracted' as they are in ways inextricable from gender. The attempt to subtract race and class elevates white, middle-class experience into the norm, making it the prototypical experience" (Grillo, 2013, p. 19).

Jennifer's tale also brings to the light hypersexualization of the Black girl body and frame (Nunn, 2016) in which the Black adolescent girl form is perceived as "loose" and "wanton" and therefore can be touched at any time without permission as the boys do within in the tale. Although she does not want this attention and asks for help, the help is denied indicating that this fate has been long accepted. Furthermore, Jennifer reiterates the cry for help again within the classroom setting and once again, the request for assistance is denied. This lack of action and silence is a concrete example of the routine violence occurring within school settings. Refusal to acknowledge racist or discriminatory actions sends the resounding message this is acceptable behavior and that one is deserving of such treatment. To do so repeatedly, erases pride and as both CRT and Black Feminist Theory tell us to name our truths, we must admit that these occurrences are not happenstance. They are the permanent and enduring legacy of racism, racial realism in action. In truth, "these systemic injustices have been designed and perpetrated to keep black people—and any other minority, oppressed, vulnerable—in fear with no sense of human value or dignity" (Missio Alliance, 2015). This is why bearing witness to Jennifer's story in our truth space is so important because if we do not openly acknowledge and discuss these issues we are essentially pushing our Black girls out of the classrooms and schools across this nation (Morris, 2016, 2019).

Incident Revamped: Countee Cullen's Experience in 2015

Amir provided another example of enduring racism as an example of life as a Black girl. Amir's story was told as tears slipped soundlessly down her cheeks. It was the story of being called a nigger. After her story, I declared, "It's like *Incident* all over again." The girls had never heard the poem and I quickly pulled it up on my phone and read it to them:

> The Incident by Countee Cullen
> Once riding in old Baltimore/

> Heart-filled, head-filled with glee; /
> I saw a Baltimorean/
> Keep looking straight at me. /
>
> Now I was eight and very small, /
> And he was no whit bigger, /
> And so I smiled, but he poked out/
> His tongue, and called me, "Nigger."/
>
> I saw the whole of Baltimore/
> From May until December; /
> Of all the things that happened there/
> That's all that I remember/
> (Cullen, 2013).

After hearing the poem, Kelsey replied, "Yup. It's just like that.... Just remixed for now" This seemed a perfect title and idea for the poem. For the poem's construction, I needed to analyze Cullen's writing to discern its stylistic elements. The setting transformed from Baltimore to the hallways of Houston. The event featured children; only instead of being eight, these were knowledgeable eighth-grade students. Both poems audaciously use the word, "Nigger." This was done because racial insults are widespread and are channels through which discriminatory actions are learned.

Delgado (1982) argued racial insults are designed to communicate the message that one's race is tied to their merit, dignity, and status and notes how these messages are passed from one generation to the next, color all of our interactions, and are therefore ingrained in our institutions. To illuminate this point, I chose to add another stanza to the poem. This stanza came from data in which Amir confessed that she did not tell any teachers about this painful incident. When I inquired as to why, she looked me in my eyes and said, "Who would believe me?" I knew this line had to be added to the poem. It needed to connect the reader to the idea that this incident impacted Amir's learning not just on the date it occurred, but is a permanent psychological and emotional scar, which may forever cloud the way she views schools.

Enabling the System: A Cry for Help Denied

As we discussed the issues of racism, a reoccurring pattern emerged: the presence and power of silence. Many times, the girls would ask teachers, in particular, Black teachers, for assistance and their requests were ignored. This fact reached a climax when, after hearing Melody's story about African American girls being treated differently when it comes to clothing. Melody did as we often instruct students to do and sought a teacher to be her advocate but was denied. Upon the story's conclusion, Marie yelled out, "So how many times we 'posed to act for help? How many times they gonna ignore us?" Marie's frustration was echoed by the other Blue Diamond Girls and I realized this event needed a poem of its own; a poem which used Marie's words, "how many times?" as a rhetorical device. Thus, the poem is a composite made up of stories from each of the Diamonds. Jennifer declared, "I'm tired of asking for help" and prompted the line, "my voice grows hoarse." Amir's declaration was, "They keep telling us 'life ain't fair,'" like I don't know that. Like I wasn't born Black and a girl." Kelsey built on the idea of equality by stating, "Yeah. Like we don't get that when they shut the door on us."

The poem lay dormant within the transcriptions. Like a farmer, I harvested their examples until the final poem, was created. The poem speaks to the power of silence which occurs when teachers refuse to acknowledge or challenge discriminatory acts which occur within schools. The silence, which is inaction, is a concrete example of racial violence and racial realism. For students, remaining silent in the face of racist and discriminatory treatment is to condone the action and its perpetrator and reifies an oppressive construct (Delgado, 1982; Missio Alliance, 2015; Morris, 2016). Even more, this practice harms both students and teachers of Color who feel they must remain silent to uphold the practice, protect their professional name, and maintain financial security. This dual infliction requires a sustained action and loving space to heal it. Silence is not the answer. Instead, we must courageously utilize truth spaces such as this one to confront racism and bigotry in open and ongoing conversations in which we explicitly discuss and examine race (Boutte, 2015; King & Swartz, 2015).

A Pocket Full of Wishes: Attracting the Opposite Sex

Embedded within the experiences of racism and gender bias was yet another intersection: the adolescent battles of desire and attraction which also conflated the intersections with issues of size. Like many girls their age, the Blue Diamonds revealed conflicts with body dissatisfaction. They believed having an "ideal" body would lead to higher self-esteem and peer status (O'Brien, Latner, Ebneter, & Hunter, 2012). Each girl had a "pocket full of wishes," they would like to change. The confessions prompted a journal topic where girls were asked to identify, if any, the aspects of their body they loved and identify, if any, the aspects of their body they would like to change. Table 6.5 displays their responses.

Their responses revealed once again the perception of the Black girl form as an object of desire; whose singular purpose is to attract attention. This is not a new idea as the majority of the representations of Black women in popular culture are firmly grounded in the dominant ideologies surrounding Black womanhood (i.e. jezebel, mammy, or baby momma) which pervades American society (Cox, 2020; Jacobs, 2016). As a cultural and historical artifact, the Black woman's body exemplifies the complexities of race and gender. Collins (1991) argued that these controlling images of Black girl sexuality pervade American

TABLE 6.5 Body Satisfaction/Dissatisfaction Responses

What I Would Keep/Change About My Body									
Kelsey		Jennifer		Amir		Melody		Marie	
Keep	Change	Keep	Change	Keep	Change	Keep	Change	Keep	Change
Butt	Breast Size	Face	Butt	Butt	Arms	Hair	Breasts Bigger	Every-thing Else	Hair
Face Shape	Skin tone	Body Shape	Skin tone	Skin tone	Legs	Face	Booty		Nails
Smile	Nose		Hair						Skin tone
Foot Size	(too big)		Hands						
			Feet						
			Lips (too big)						

society to legitimize the continued marginalization of Black women. Its effects can clearly be seen in the girls' responses. They each wanted to alter their body not for themselves but to attract a partner. Although the girls all wanted to make changes, they questioned if these changes would alter their personhood. This thought is reiterated through the last line of the poem, which asks a rhetorical question, "If I'm all of those things, would I still be me?" This question remained unanswered during their discussion; therefore, it was purposefully left as the last line so the reader could continue pondering its value just as the Blue Diamond girls and I did.

What Is Body Image?

The poem *What Is Body Image?* was formed from the girls' journal responses to the same question and stands as an important element in findings on intersectionality. Their answers revealed a nuanced understanding of the complexities of body image. The girls quickly noted it was more than just size but an amalgamation of how an individual perceives size, skin tone, weight, height, hair length, hair type, eye color, and eye size. They also recognized this definition could change from day to day or in some cases hour to hour. This knowledge of body image does not dissuade conflicts which occur indicating differing perceptions on body image. For this reason, this poem serves as a precursor to the *Blessings upon Blessings* poem which reveals such a conflict in action.

Blessings upon Blessings

One topic about which the Blue Diamond girls were particularly passionate was the discrimination they face due to their body shape and size. This is a topic which is currently having much discussion throughout the nation (Chang, 2016; Morris, 2016). Yet, if a Black Feminist lens is not applied, it is easy to overlook how this rule enforcement disproportionately affects young Black girls. The Blue Diamond girls each provided several examples of being sent to In-School Suspension for refusing to change their clothing. Many times, the girls were told to call home and their parents or guardians refused to bring clothing to school as they felt that the clothing *did* meet school regulations, but it was their daughters' body which did not. Kelsey elucidated this premise by describing an encounter between her and Houston's principal. Although Kelsey and her white classmate Mary Alice were dressed similarly, the principal told Kelsey her clothes were too revealing while complimenting Mary Alice on her outfit.

Scholars offer this discrimination which occurs repeatedly harkens back to the hypersexualization of the Black girl form from the time of colonization and enslavement when Black women were stereotyped as "jezebels" and "loose" as a way to justify their rapes (Morris, 2016). This is one of many examples of racial realism in action – a concept of which the Blue Diamond girls were clearly aware. Due to this long-standing and unchecked bias, many Black girls are sent home for clothing which is deemed too promiscuous (Morris, 2016). Incidents such as this fuel anger and distrust but also add to increased suspensions and expulsion for Black girls throughout the country. According to the African-American Policy Forum (2014), while Black boys are the groups most likely to be suspended from school, Black girls have a higher relative risk – six times higher – of suspension in comparison to their white counterparts. Even more, if girls, like Kelsey in this case, try to defend themselves, they are further labeled "rude" or "defiant." The girls are placed in a no-win situation, where they must silently accept their fate or be further penalized. Kelsey decided to rebel by selecting to go to in-school suspension. Instead of being praised for her abilities to speak out against injustice, she instead is chastised by her Black teachers and told to change next time indicating this is a battle that she would not win. This was illuminated in the poem using the lines, "I know we will battle once more." For Kelsey, sanctuary did not come within the normal hours of the school day. Instead, sanctuary came from her truth space after school as we boldly confronted and discussed these issues.

Researcher's Note: Examining Intersectionalities

Identity is a complex thing and the poems within this theme speak to this fact. Yet, there is a power and hope when we examine the junctures of identities. I tried to do that in this poem illuminating my reflections on the data and the literature, reflecting on intersectionalities as foundations for creating liberatory and empowering communities. Collins argued (1991) that within these spaces:

> Black women and men are nurtured to confront oppressive social institutions. Power from this perspective is a creative power used for the good of the community, whether that community is conceptualized as one's family, church community, or the next generation of the community's children. By making the community stronger, African American women become empowered, and that same community can serve as a source of support when Black women encounter race, gender, and class oppression.
>
> (p. 221)

The Blue Diamond girls did not need prodding to reveal their stories. They only needed to be invited to share them by a learner who was willing to create a space in which they would critically listen to their truths, and center learning around their realities. I wanted to end the intersectionality section by applauding the honest confessions which came forth in our truth space. I did not expect the girls to respond, "Thank you for asking," but their response reiterated the necessity of our sister circle and I wanted this fact to linger with the reader.

Combating White Supremacy, Gender Bias, and Sizism Using Counternarratives

A methodological approach popularized by Critical Race Theorists, the counternarrative is a powerful pedagogical tool to "challenge majoritarian stories rooted in a dominant Eurocentric perspective that justify social inequities and normalize white superiority and thus, white supremacy" (Huber, 2008, p. 187). This section of Chapter 5 was critical to my articulation of findings. Hooks (1995) argued that the "history of Black liberation movements in the United States could be characterized as a struggle over images as much as it has also been a struggle for rights, for equal access" (p. 57). The counternarrative privileges experiential knowledge and the stories from people of Color which often go untold (Delgado, Stefancic, & Harris, 2017). In the face of popular media which reifies stereotypical representations of the mammy, jezebel, and the baby mama, the counternarrative serves as a dismantling tool and a symbolic mirror displaying the beauty, strength, courage, and resilience of a people.

I engaged the students in writing counternarratives by first studying picture books that are counternarratives. We studied *Hair Dance!* (Johnson, 2007), *My People* (Hughes & Smith, 2009), and *Dancing in the Wings* (Allen, 2000). These titles were also chosen because of their availability in Houston's Media Center. The girls read the titles to each other and discussed the various ways we communicate our stories and how the images which appeared in the book contrasted with many which appear in rap videos and social media. They quickly grasped this was "all about love" and "inspiration." They compiled a list of the ways on the dry erase board and decided which forms would be the best to convey messages of love. They finally decided on photography, poetry, music, and praise dance. Each research partner decided that they should be a leader over a particular section. Jennifer took the lead on photography, Marie on poetry, Melody on music, and Kelsey and Amir co-chaired leading the praise dance. Time was devoted for the girls to create their counternarratives or as Marie coined them "our celebration stories." Since storytelling has a long historical and literary heritage in the African American community, it only makes sense that it is the perfect tool to ensure survival, empowerment, and liberation (Bell, 1992; Boutte, 2015; Grant, Brown, & Brown, 2015; King & Swartz, 2015).

Counternarratives: A Definition Poem

I developed this poem from my review of the literature surrounding counternarratives drawing from work in CRT. Solorzano and Yosso (2002) introduced counterstorytelling or counternarratives as valuable tools for educational research and classroom practice. They defined them as ways of telling the stories of people who are traditionally silenced or marginalized to examine, challenge, and critique master or dominant narratives. They identified three main types of counternarratives: personal stories, other people's stories, and composite stories.

Counternarratives serve several distinct purposes; they (a) build and sustain a community for people often marginalized and overlooked; (b) critique/challenge commonly held ideas or notions; (c) create a new perspective into reality; (d) open possibilities; and (e) combine current reality with open possibilities to create a new rich world (Delgado, 2014). As such, this poem embodies my challenge to the Blue Diamond girls to create counternarratives for Black girls who are struggling with the unbearable burden of weight, race, and gender.

Naming Myself: A Body Visual Poem

This visual poem came into being in one afternoon after Marie was chastised by a teacher for being rude. When she came into the group, she was visibly angry. As a group, we hugged her and asked her to explain her anger. She stated during the snack and homework time, a boy had "called her out her name," meaning that he had used a derogatory term. Marie boldly countered his remark by saying, "If you want to call me som'thing… call me Black and beautiful 'cause besides my name, that's the only thing I'm answering to." The girls agreed with her and began to yell out other things people could call them such as "intelligent," or "bold" or "courageous." After creating the list, Kelsey looked pointedly at me and said,

> You know what… Forget all those posters they got hanging all over the school. You know what Black girls need… They need this poster 'cause ain't nobody got time for some ignant person callin' people out they name.

As a group, they decided to design a poster which takes pride in self-love and affirmation. Jennifer served as a graphic design artist and masterfully negotiated the myriad of ideas which arose, ideas which ultimately became this poem. In the end, they decided to feature themselves, the symbolic mirror, and the words by which they have every right to be called: Black, beautiful, intelligent, courageous, and bold.

Fat: A Counternarrative in Visual Form

This poem stands in contrast to the poem in the introductory section, *Fat: A Visual Poem*. Contrast occurs in both the stance of visual and the words which comprise it. This visual does not display a person who is embarrassed by size; instead, this individual proudly loves her shape and takes a defiant and fashionable pose. Melody decided that girls needed a "Power Playlist" a list of songs which inspire and motivate. She challenged each girl to find an artist, a song, and a featured stanza. The visual includes lines from each of the featured stanzas. Table 6.6 displays the artists, songs, and the featured stanzas.

The playlist and words of love were designed to deconstruct the language of war surrounding fat and obesity. Immersing students in creating this type of text helped to nurture and represent the elements of our experience that were liberating and humanizing.

TABLE 6.6 Power Playlist

Artist	Song:	Featured Stanza:
Beyoncé	"Move Your Body"	I ain't worried doing me tonight A little sweat ain't never hurt nobody While you all standin' on the wall I'm the one tonight Getting bodied, getting bodied, getting bodied, getting bodied
Christina Aguilera	"Beautiful"	I am beautiful No matter what they say Words can't bring me down I am beautiful In every single way Yes words can't bring me down Oh no So don't you bring me down today
Keri Hilson	"Pretty Girl Rock"	All eyes on me when I walk in No question that this girl's a ten Don't hate me cause I'm beautiful Don't hate me cause I'm beautiful My walk, my talk, the way I dress It's not my fault so please don't trip Don't hate me cause I'm beautiful
Britt Nicole	"Gold"	This, this is for all the girls, boys all over the world Whatever you've been told, you're worth more than gold So hold your head up high, it's your time to shine From the inside out it shows, you're worth more than gold (Gold gold, you're gold) You're worth more than gold (Gold gold, you're gold)
Chila Lynn	"Real Woman"	She ain't made for those magazines full of photoshop queens telling her how she should be. Oh there's no doubt about it she's as real as a woman can be.

Greater Is Coming: Praise in Lyrics and Movement

Amir and Kelsey decided that praise dance was an effective counternarrative "because sometimes there are no words. Sometimes you gotta just move." In truth, praise dances have been incorporated as a part of the Black Christian ministry to "praise the Lord; for his mercy endureth forever" (2 Chr. 20, 21, KJV). Yet, even this act serves as a site of resistance indicating praise can occur in many different forms of dance. Dance is more than mere movement; it is a political act to speak out against injustice (Valadez, 2012). The girls choose to dance to "Greater is Coming" by Jekalyn Carr. When asked why this song was selected, Kelsey replied, "Right now being fat or overweight means you are teased or laughed at, but it want always be this way. You have to love yourself and believe that one day all bodies will be respected." Kelsey's response demonstrates a radically simple idea: We are all worthy of love and self-respect. If every culture has capital, then surely every body has worth (Yosso, 2005).

Body Love: An Autobiography in Five Short Chapters

The final counternarrative is a collection of five photographs with inspirational thoughts. This poem challenges *Fat: Autobiography in Five Chapters* as it discusses what is needed to accept and love the body. When I asked Melody why she selected photographs she stated, "Pictures are important." Her reply is quite profound. Images, especially affirming images, are necessary for survival and liberation. As hooks (1995) argued:

> Though rarely articulated as such, the camera became [and is] a political instrument, a way to resist misrepresentation as well as a means by which Alternative images could be produced. Photography… offered the possibility of immediate intervention, useful in the production of counterhegemonic representations even as it was also an instrument of pleasure. The camera allowed Black folks to coming image-making, resistance struggle, and pleasure.
> (p. 60)

Each research partner created an affirmation. As a group, they scouted locations and backdrops for the pictures and shifted roles as photographers. Observing them as they completed this process was affirming for me as a researcher indicating it speaks to the power of research as activism – creating responsible activists who desire to change the world. The girls used their images to offer words of strength needed to dismantle a language of hate surrounding race, size, and gender. Their closing thoughts are powerful and poignant: Respect all bodies, know your worth, live without negative thoughts, be at peace, and most importantly, love yourself.

Truthful Transparency: Reflecting on Writing

Writing this chapter and the verse novel that precedes it was a war with words and emotion. I felt myself bleeding onto the page. It took me back to the passion and emotion of the experience that was this truth space. Collectively, the Blue Diamond girls and I cried an ocean of tears; much needed as there was healing and catharsis in the pain. We found solace and sanctuary in our truth space, in our knowledge, in our common experiences. That is perhaps the most significant finding of all: That truth spaces such as this can provide support and sanctuary that no other space in the school provides. The research is clear. Middle School can often be filled with restrictive classroom environments (Erigha & Crooks-Allen, 2020) with teachers who exhibit low expectations, present irrelevant curriculum, and refuse to provide support (Morris, 2016). Like Woodson (1933) stated, this is not education but indoctrination not only for students of Color but for white students who leave schooling convinced of their superiority. The goal of education should be to foster critically and culturally conscious citizens who actively seek to transform the world (Freire, 2000). In this case, the truth space was a sister circle which provided a sanctuary for the Blue Diamond girls to challenge hegemonic beauty ideals which endured for centuries. Being a member of this community afforded solidarity to live and love our Blackness.

As I wrote the poems and this chapter explaining that process, I also realized this was yet another layer of analysis – the acts of reflecting on and articulating what we had done illuminated the kindredness between the Blue Diamond Girls, me, and our ancestors; our poetry was a co-construction building upon a rich literary and activist heritage. We are but the fruits from a rich soil of wisdom. By standing on their shoulders, we were able to see a better future. For this reason, I close this chapter paying homage to those whose words are our roots and anchors (Figure 6.4). To our literary and activist past which redeemed us in our present and secures promise in our future… we say Ashe!

FIGURE 6.4 Black Literary Heritage

References

Acevedo, E. (2018). *The poet X: A novel.* Harper Teen, an imprint of Harper Collins.
Ainsworth, J. (2013). What's wrong with pink pearls and cornrow braids? Employee dress codes and the semiotic performance of race and gender in the workplace. *Law, Culture and Visual Studies,* 241–260.
Allen, D. (2000). *Dancing in the wings.* Dial Books for Young Readers.
Anfara, V. A., Brown, K. M., & Mangione, T. L. (2002). Qualitative analysis on stage: making the research process more public. *Educational Researcher, 31*(7), 28–38.
Angelou, M. (1970). *I know why the caged bird sings.* Random House.
Baker-Bell, A. (2020). *Linguistic justice: Black language, literacy, identity, and pedagogy.* Routledge.
Baldwin, J. (1961). The Negro in American culture. *Cross Currents, 11*(3), 205–224.
Beale, F. (1971). *Double jeopardy: To be Black and female.* Radical Education Project.
Beauboeuf-Lafontant, T. (2003). Strong and large Black women?: Exploring relationships between deviant womanhood and weight. *Gender & Society, 17*(1), 112.
Beers, G. K., & Probst, R. E. (2013). *Notice & note: Strategies for close reading.* Heinemann.
Bell, D. (1992). *Faces at the bottom of the well: The permanence of racism.* Basic Books.
Bergner, G. (2009). Black children, white preference: Brown v. Board, the Doll Tests, and the politics of self-esteem. *American Quarterly, 61*(2), 299–332.
Bishop, R. S. (2007). *Free within ourselves: The development of African American children's literature.* Greenwood Press.
Blackmon, C. M. (2009). *Routed sisterhood black American female identity and the black female community* (Doctoral dissertation, Ohio State University) [Abstract].
Bonilla-Silva, E., & Ray, V. (2008). When Whites love a Black leader: Race matters in Obamerica. *Journal of African American Studies, 13*(2), 176–183.
Boutte, G. (2015). *Educating African American students: And how are the children?* Routledge.
Chang, C. (2016). How Black girls are locked out of America's schools. *The New Republic.* https://newrepublic.com/article/136390/birth-conservative-media-know
Channsin-Berry, D., & Duke, B. (Directors). (2011). *Dark girls* [Video file]. One Village Entertainment, Distributed by RLJ Entertainment.
Collins, P. H. (1991). *Black feminist thought: Knowledge, consciousness, and the politics of empowerment.* Routledge.
Collins, P. H. (1998). *Fighting words: Black women and the search for justice.* University of Minnesota Press.
Collins, P. H. (2000). *Black feminist thought: Knowledge, consciousness, and the politics of empowerment.* Routledge.
Cook, D. A. (2013). Blurring the boundaries: The mechanics of creating composite characters. In M. Lynn & A. Dixson (Eds.), *Handbook of critical race theory in education: CRT and innovations in educational research methodologies* (pp. 181–194). Routledge.
Cox, J. (2020). *Fat girls in black bodies: Creating communities of our own.* North Atlantic Books.
Crenshaw, K. (1989). Demarginalizing the intersection of race and sex: A black feminist critique of antidiscrimination doctrine, feminist theory and antiracist politics. *The University of Chicago Legal Forum,* 139–167.
Cullen, C. (2013). *Collected poems.* Amistad Research Center.
Dawkins, R. (1976). *The selfish gene.* Oxford University Press.
Delgado, R. (1982). Words that wound: A tort action for racial insults, epithets, and name-calling. *Harvard Civil Rights-Civil Liberties Law Review, 17,* 133–181.
Delgado, R. (2000). Derrick Bell's toolkit --Fit to dismantle that famous house. *New York University Law Review, 75*(2), 283–307.

Delgado, R. (2014). *Critical race theory: An introduction* (2nd ed.). New York University Press.
Delgado, R., Stefancic, J., & Harris, A. P. (2017). *Critical race theory: An introduction*. New York University Press.
Eisner, E. W. (1991). *The enlightened eye: Qualitative inquiry and the enhancement of educational practice*.
Erigha, M., & Crooks-Allen, A. (2020). Digital communities of Black girlhood: New media technologies and online discourses of empowerment. *The Black Scholar, 50*(4), 66–76. doi:10.1080/00064246.2020.1811601
Fisher, M. T. (2005). From the coffee house to the school house: The promise and potential of spoken word poetry in school contexts. *English Education, 37*, 115–131.
Fleischman, P., & Beddows, E. (1988). *Joyful noise: Poems for two voices*. Harper & Row.
Foucault, M. (1978). *The history of sexuality*. Vintage.
Freire, P. (2000). *Pedagogy of the oppressed. Continuum*.
Freire, P., & Macedo, D. P. (1987). *Literacy: Reading the word and the world*. Bergin & Garvey.
Garnett, J. (2020, July). *Love is a parable*. https://loveisaparable.com/cofounder-loveadvocate
Gatewood, B. J., & Norris, A. N. (2019). Silencing prisoner protests: Criminology, black women and state-sanctioned violence. *Decolonization of Criminology and Justice, 1*(1), 52–77.
Gay, G. (2010). *Culturally responsive teaching: Theory, research, and practice*. Teachers College Press.
Gonzalez, L., & González Ybarra, M. (2020). Multimodal cuentos as fugitive literacies on the MEXICO-US borderlands. *English Education, 52*(3), 223–255.
González, N., Moll, L. C., & Amanti, C. (2009). *Funds of knowledge: Theorizing practices in households, communities, and classrooms*. Routledge.
Gordon, C. T., Council, T., Dukes, N., & Muhammad, G. E. (2019). Defying the single narrative of black girls' literacies: A narrative inquiry exploring an african american read-in. *Multicultural Perspectives, 21*(1), 3–10. doi:10.1080/15210960.2019.1572484
Grant, C. A., Brown, K. D., & Brown, A. L. (2015). *Black intellectual thought in education: The missing traditions of Anna Julia Cooper, Carter G. Woodson, and Alain Leroy Locke*. Routledge.
Griffin, R. A. (2016). Black Female Faculty, Resilient Grit, and Determined Grace or "Just because everything is different doesn't mean anything has changed". *The Journal of Negro Education, 85*(3), 365–379.
Grillo, T. (2013). Anti-essentialism and intersectionality: Tools to dismantle the master's house. *Berkeley Journal of Gender, Law & Justice, 10*(1), 16–30.
Harris, C. I. (1993). Whiteness as property. *Harvard Law Review, 106*(8), 1707–1791.
Harrison, J., Macgibbon, L., & Morton, M. (2001). Regimes of trustworthiness in qualitative research: The rigors of reciprocity. *Qualitative Inquiry, 7*(3), 323–345.
Hines, K., & Cass, J. (2011). *The power of internet memes and a lot of fun along the way*. Retrieved from http://1stwebdesigner.com/power-internet-memes/
hooks, B. (1992). *Black looks: Race and representation*. South End Press.
hooks, B. (1995). *Killing rage: Ending racism*. Holt, Henry & Company, Inc.
hooks, B. (2012). *All about love: New visions*. William Morrow.
Huber, L. (2008). Building critical race methodologies in educational research: A research note on critical race Testimonio. *FIU Law Review, 4*(1), 167
Hughes, L., & Smith, C. R. (2009). *My people*. Atheneum Books for Young Readers Books.
Hunter, M. (2007). The persistent problem of colorism: Skin tone, status, and inequality. *Sociology Compass, 1*(1), 237–254.

Jacobs, C. E. (2016). Developing the "Oppositional Gaze": Using Critical Media Pedagogy and Black Feminist Thought to Promote Black Girls' Identity Development. *The Journal of Negro Education, 85*(3), 225–238.

Janssen, I., Craig, W. M., Boyce, W. F., & Pickett, W. (2004). Associations between overweight and obesity with bullying behaviors in school-aged children. *Pediatrics, 113*(5), 1187–1194.

Johnson, D. (2007). *Hair dance!* Henry Holt.

Johnson, L. L., Boutte, G., Greene, G., & Smith, D. E. (2018). *African diaspora literacy: The heart of transformation in K-12 schools and teacher education.* Lexington Books, an imprint of The Rowman & Littlefield Publishing Group.

Jordan, J. (1977). *Things that I do in the dark: Selected poetry.* Random House.

Jordan, J. (1986). The difficult miracle of Black poetry in America or something like a sonnet for Phillis Wheatley. *The Massachusetts Review, 27*(2), 252–262.

Hankivsky, O. (2014). *Intersectionality 101* (Rep., pp. 1–36). The Institute for Intersectionality Research & Policy.

King, J. E., & Swartz, E. (2015). *The Afrocentric praxis of teaching for freedom: Connecting culture to learning.* Routledge.

Kinloch, V. (2005). Poetry, literacy, and creativity: Fostering effective learning strategies in an urban classroom. *English Education, 37*, 96–114.

Kleon, A. (2010). *Newspaper blackout.* Harper Perennial.

Kohli, R., Johnson, R. N., & Perez, L. H. (2006). Naming racism: A conceptual look at internalized racism in U.S. schools. *Chicano-Latino Law Review, 25*, 183–206.

Kress, G. R. (2003). *Literacy in the new media age.* Routledge.

Ladenheim, M. (2014). Engaging honors students through newspaper blackout poetry. *National Collegiate Honors Council, 10*, 45–54.

Love, B. (2020). *We want to do more than survive: Abolitionist teaching and the pursuit of educational freedom.* Beacon Press.

Lorde, A. (1984). *Sister outsider: Essays and speeches.* Crossing Press.

Missio Alliance. (2015). *On violence and living in a 'racialized' society: Silence sends a clear message when we have an opportunity to act.* http://www.missioalliance.org/on-violence-and-living-in-a-"racialized"-society-silence-sends-a-clear-message-when-we-have-an-opportunity-to-act/

Morris, M. W. (2016). *Pushout: The criminalization of Black girls in schools.* The New Press.

Morris, M. W. (2019). *Sing a rhythm, dance a blues: Education for the liberation of Black and Brown girls.* The New Press.

Morrison, T. (1984). Memory, creation, and writing. *Thought, 59*(4), 385–390.

Morrison, T. (1994). *The bluest eye.* Plume Book.

Muhammad, G. (2020). *Cultivating genius: An equity framework for culturally and historically responsive literacy.* Scholastic.

Murray, S. (2007). Corporeal knowledges and deviant bodies: Perceiving the fat body. *Social Semiotics, 17*(3), 361–373.

Murray, S. (2008). Pathologizing "fatness": Medical authority and popular culture. *Sociology of Sport Journal, 25*(1), 7–21.

Nash, J. C. (2013). Practicing love: Black feminism, love-politics, and post-intersectionality. *Meridians, 11*(2), 1–24.

Nelson, P. (1989). *There's a hole in my sidewalk: The romance of self-discovery.* Beyond Words Pub.

Nichter, M. (2000). *Fat talk: What girls and their parents say about dieting.* Harvard University Press.

Nunn, N. M. (2016). Super-girl: Strength and sadness in Black girlhood. *Gender and Education, 30*(2), 239–258. doi:10.1080/09540253.2016.1225013

O'Brien, K. S., Latner, J. D., Ebneter, D., & Hunter, J. A. (2012). Obesity discrimination: The role of physical appearance, personal ideology, and anti-fat prejudice. *International Journal of Obesity, 37*(3), 455–460.

Oliver, J. E. (2006). *Fat politics: The real story behind America's obesity epidemic*. Oxford University Press.

Overweight and Obesity Statistics (Ser. 4158, pp. 1–6, Issue brief No. 4). (2012). The National Institute of Diabetes and Digestive and Kidney Diseases.

Robinson, M. (2000). *Your mercy* [CD]. Metairie.

Rosenblatt, L. M. (1978). *The reader, the text, the poem: The transactional theory of the literary work*. Southern Illinois University Press.

Russell-Cole, K., Wilson, M., & Hall, R. E. (2013). *The color complex: The politics of skin color in a new millennium*. Anchor Books.

Schott Foundation for Public Education. (2016). *The urgency of now: The Schott 50 state report on public education and Black males*. (Rep.). Cambridge University Press.

Schott, N. D. (2016). Race, online space and the feminine: Unmapping 'Black Girl Thinspiration'. *Critical Sociology, 43* (7–8), 1029–1043.

Solorzano, D. G., & Yosso, T. J. (2001). Critical race and Lat Crit theory and method: Counter-storytelling. *International Journal of Qualitative Studies in Education, 14*(4), 471–495.

Solorzano, D. G., & Yosso, T. J. (2002). Critical race methodology: Counter-storytelling as an analytical framework for education research. *Qualitative Inquiry, 8*(1), 23–44

Taylor, S. R. (2018). *The body is not an apology: The power of radical self-love*. Berrett-Koehler.

Townsend, T. G., Thomas, A. J., & Jackson-Lowman, H. (2013). Jezebel's legacy: The development of African American heterosexual girls' emerging sexuality in the context of oppressive images and the armoring influence of mother-daughter relationships. In H. Jackson-Lowman (Ed.), *Afrikan American women: Living at the crossroads of race, gender, class, and culture*. Cognella Academic Publishing.

Valadez, V. (2012). *Dancing Amoxtli: Danza Azteca and indigenous body art as forms of resistance* (Doctoral dissertation, Abstract, California State University). Retrieved from http://scholarworks.calstate.edu/bitstream/handle/10211.2/1182/WHOLETHESIS.pdf?sequence=1

Waters, B. S. M., Evans-Winters, V. E., & Love, B. L. (2019). *Celebrating twenty years of black girlhood: The Lauryn Hill Reader (Urban Girls Book 2)* (1st ed.). Peter Lang Inc., International Academic Publishers.

Weiss, J., & Herndon, S. (2001). *Brave new voices: The youth speaks guide to teaching spoken-word poetry*. Heinemann.

Williams, B., & Zenger, A. A. (2012). *New media literacies and participatory popular culture across borders*. Routledge.

Woodson, C. G. (1933). *The miseducation of the Negro*. Africa World Press.

Woodson, K. (2020). *Colorism: Investigating a global phenomenon colorism: Investigating a global phenomenon*. Fielding University Press.

Yosso, T. J. (2005). Whose culture has capital? A critical race theory discussion of community cultural wealth. *Race Ethnicity and Education, 8*(1), 69–91.

7

"QUIET AS IT'S KEPT"

Teachers as Truth Warriors Moving Forward with Urgency

odo nyera

FOR TRACEY

She looked inside her.
Deep inside.
To the dark parts.
the parts hidden by shadow; Cloaked in mystique.
She reached through
the cobwebs and
touched places of pain.
Wounds that time forgot.
Pulsing and raw,
She held them in hand.
Kissed them,
and whispered, "Thank you."
For they fueled her passion,
Fortified her strength.
They had made her a Warrior.
And as she looked toward the sun,
Mother Earth smiled.

Dywanna Smith, 2020

When I began this foray into writing about truth spaces, I knew I needed to surround myself with wisdom and inspiration. To do so, I created a vision board – a place which would radiate positivity and center my focus and thoughts. My vision board (Figure 7.1) was a collage of words and images which had comforted me through the decades. When I stared at it, I saw faces and stories like mine because I'd centered my vision on insight from Black women authors who

DOI: 10.4324/9780429340161-7

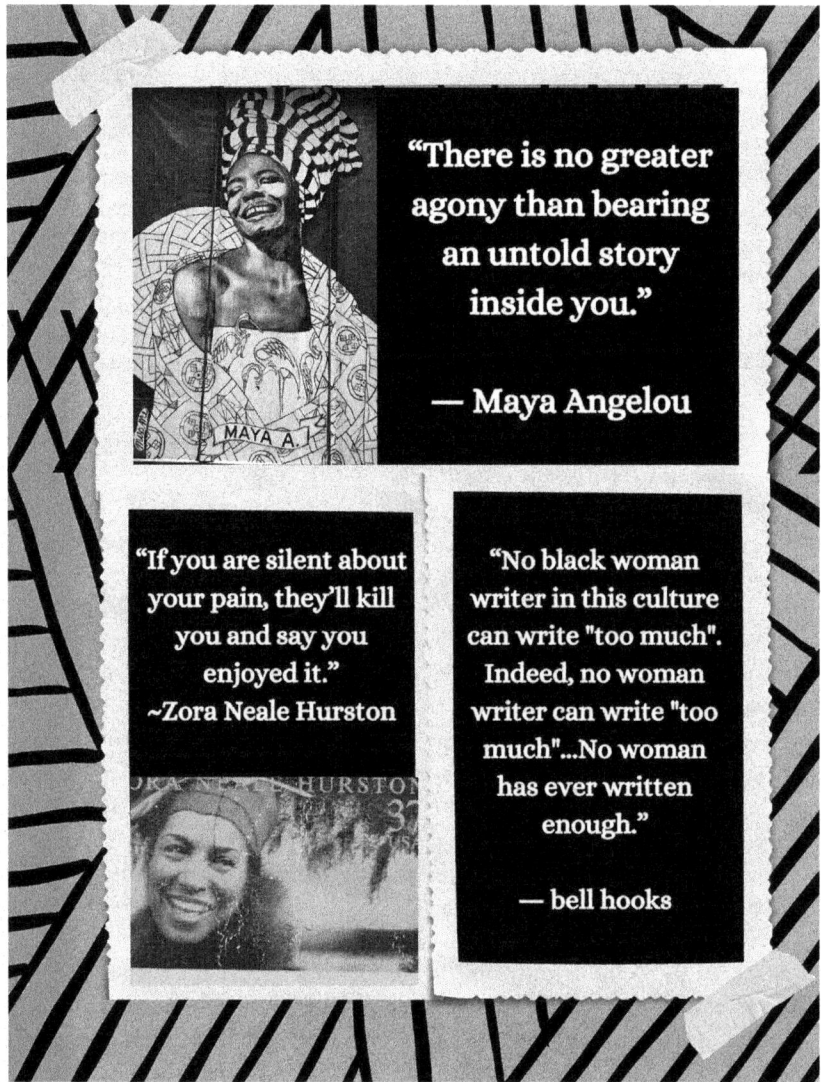

FIGURE 7.1 "If you are silent about your pain": Contextualizing Implications

had nourished my spirit through depression, trauma, and grief. I repeated their words until I was able to formulate my own. They were, and are, my core; they are my wisdom warriors. As the words of wisdom also embody the struggle of the Blue Diamond girls, it seems only fitting that these words ground my concluding thoughts and implications for practice and teachers as truth warriors.

Consulting my Black literary heritage was again critical as I titled this chapter. I chose the opening words from Toni Morrison's *The Bluest Eye* (1994) – "quiet as it's kept." Morrison uses these words to draw readers into the cloud of secrecy surrounding the horrific realities within the Breedlove family. Pecola's life was either discussed in whispers or never discussed at all. The words struck me as both powerful and prophetic as they can be used to describe the realities of Black Adolescent girls. Black girls' lives which are so often "quiet as it's kept," are rarely discussed or acknowledged. But if transformation is to occur, these truths cannot be hidden. Instead, they should serve as testimony and scaffolding to securing academic, social, and cultural equity. Therefore, I will not keep their words quiet.

> "If you are silent about your pain, they'll kill you and say you enjoyed it."
> ~ Zora Neale Hurston

Throughout our nation, Black girls are being brutalized (Schott Foundation for Public Education, 2016). The Spring Valley Incident, which occurred after the Blue Diamond Truth Space, was a vivid and very local example of the routine dehumanization which occurs against Black girls and it clearly demonstrated the need for humanizing, critical, and creative truth spaces for young Black girls to be heard, refuged, validated, understood, and supported. The story of this "incident" is an important preface to this discussion of why and how this research into truth spaces as a pedagogical practice is a vital necessity in the lives of the Blue Diamonds and of young Black women everywhere.

For me, October 26, 2015, began as a normal day. I sat in my office diligently working at my desk. My colleagues and I anxiously prepared for impending professional development sessions or curriculum development. The room was a cacophony of voices brainstorming ideas, the soft clicks and clacks of the keyboard, and the quiet squeaks of a dry erase marker as it treads across the surface of chart paper. I was lost in the thoughts of planning when my phone rang, jarring me from my thoughts.

I picked up the phone and swiped at its screen to see a close friend's number. I paused because she was not one for calls, preferring to communicate by text. Still, I was in the zone and did not want to be disturbed. So, I gently pressed the "Remind Me Later" function and resumed working. There was a moment of silence before my phone buzzed again, this time with a text message. Although I appreciated the tenacity, I was determined to get work done; but my phone would not be dissuaded. It continued to buzz, vibrate, and ring as alerts from text messages, instant messages, and social media were updated. Immediately, my spirit became unsettled as these sounds were an orchestra of foreboding. I could only utter a quick prayer as I picked up my phone to discover what was wrong. A quick swipe revealed three to four text messages, all with the same theme: Have you seen the news? What is going on? How could this happen? The final message did not have a question; instead, it gave a firm command: **Check our local news station NOW!**

I quickly logged onto the news station and watched the disturbing video of a young Black girl being flung from her seat by a school resource officer. Her crime? Refusing to put her cell phone away. I watched the video with the cold shock of confusion, Black rage, and a deep, deep, sadness. I called my colleagues and asked if they had seen the video. As a collective group, we watched the video and after it ended, we sat in a heavy silence. My heart began to pound in my chest because experience had taught me what would come next. When mouths could once again form words, my colleagues began to voice rationalizations: "Could it have been this was a student who is known for behavioral disruptions? Could she have been defiant? Could she have threatened the teacher?" My answer to each one of these questions forcefully remained the same, "This is a child! This is someone's BABY. Why was she treated like this? NO ONE DESERVES THIS!"

Had we all stared at that video with a humanizing and critical love, my colleagues would have been equally outraged. Instead, I was met with confusion, doubt, and insipid rationalizations and justifications – for the school resource officer, not for the student. There was no cry of outrage, no concern expressed for the child, no exclamation of the many more effective ways the situation could have been handled. I was not surprised by their reactions because as an American society, we have become so inundated with images of Black and Brown bodies being violated, attacked, maligned, and brutalized, that many believe these bodies and their corresponding peoples, are exempt from humanity, equality, critical compassion and love (Beale, 1971; Boutte, 2015; Crenshaw, Ocen, & Nanda, 2015; DuBois, 1903; Hooks, 1990, 1992, 1995, 2012; Johnson, Boutte, Greene, & Smith, 2018; Johnson, Bryan, & Boutte, 2018; Love, 2020; Lyiscott, 2020; Morris, 2016, 2019; Muhammad, 2020; Ohito, 2020). White supremacy, so ingrained into the fabrics of our society, was clear to me in the brutal force used with this young woman, even in the reaction of the Black teacher who approved the action – internalized acquiescence to the supremacy of whiteness and the assumed guilt of the victim.

I do not recall the remainder of the conversation with my colleagues. I needed to make a quick escape. I quickly walked to the restroom, locked the door, and cried. For five minutes, tears softly rolled down my cheeks. It was not the cry of screams and red eyes. This was a silent cry, tears of a pain that had not yet fully been internalized. My emotional waves would not breach their dam. I whispered a prayer, wiped my cheeks, and with a grim determination, walked backed to my office. The office which was once filled with many sounds was now grimly silent. It was this eerie silence which reminded me of Zora Neale Hurston's famous words, If you are silent about your pain, they'll kill you and say you enjoyed it." If I was this emotionally stilted, I wondered about the emotional state of my research partners. I walked to my desk, picked up my phone, and began to text the Blue Diamond girls: "Are you okay? Are you willing to talk about what happened? What can I do to help?" I knew they were somewhere viewing these images and like me, they would realize that this could happen at any school in America and that this event could have easily occurred with them.

The Spring Valley Incident was repeatedly shown on news broadcasts throughout the country. We witnessed this young Black woman's dehumanization, but as a nation, we were not allowed to speak her name. Her name and her version of the story were silenced and erased. Just like the brutalities offered in this book, this was the claiming of a body by those who should have no claim to it; once again, a body was inflicted with symbolic and physical violence, but the identity, the humanity of that body was not publicly affirmed. This one incident illustrates the complexities and intersectionalities of being a Black adolescent girl in America, fraught with violence, erasure, and life in the margins. It is my hope that this book will lead to the development of truth spaces to serve as radical hope and possibility (hooks, 1992) for young Black girls in schools everywhere.

As I frantically texted my Blue Diamond Girls, I waited for a reply. I desperately wanted to know their responses to this traumatic event. The first reply I received only contained three short words, "Why? Why? Why?" Although simplistic, this message only affirmed there were questions and feelings that needed to be acknowledged, heard, and discussed. I knew the Blue Diamond girls would once again need a place to heal. Though I could not get to them face to face, our phones became a new truth space – a way to discuss communal grieving and healing. I know there are young Black women across the country experiencing the same need day after day, year after year for a variety of reasons. It is for this reason the Blue Diamond truth space provides a model – an important pedagogical tool – for liberation, catharsis, and healing.

Implications for Teachers as Truth Warriors

"There is no greater agony than bearing an untold story inside you."
~ Maya Angelou

When reflecting on her life and writing her autobiography, Maya Angelou (1970) declared, "There is no greater agony than bearing an untold story inside you." Ironically, the same words can be used to describe young Black girls who face erasure within the classroom walls, who are overlooked within the school's curriculum, and are physically attacked on the streets (Battle, 2021; Evans-Winters, 2011; Evans-Winters, 2019; Morris, 2016, 2019). In 2007, a six-year-old Black child was arrested for having a tantrum in her classroom. In 2013, an eight-year-old Black girl was arrested for reportedly "acting out" (Webb, 2013). In 2014, a Black girl in the sixth grade was almost expelled for writing the word "hi" on her locker at school (Logan, 2014). In 2015, we were deeply disturbed by a young black girl in Texas being manhandled by a police officer (Soichet, Fantz, & Yan, 2015). The stories from around the country provoke anger, sadness, and a firm resolve that change must happen now.

If we are to affect such change, then learning from Black girls and women is critical. Muhammad and Haddix (2016) postulated, "If we focus on excellent educational pedagogies for Black women and girls, given their distinct oppressive histories, then Black women lay the foundation for advancing education for all" (p. 300). Like Haddix and Muhammad, I believe Black women educators should lead the charge of transformation by establishing and maintaining humanizing, critical, and creative truth spaces such as the Blue Diamonds. By focusing on the intersectionalities of race, gender, and size, the Blue Diamond girls were able to discuss and analyze experiences of racism: the suspensions, double standards, and erasures all apparent within their middle school contexts. By standing on the shoulders of literary ancestors, they were able to discover this fight is not new and learned to cope and communicate as their ancestors did through the healing power of the arts, be it writing, music, or photography. Our truth space affirmed there is healing in the act of creation. Whether it was through hugs, discourse, critically listening, or the act of creation, truth space provided a nurturing and restorative community – a cathartic and liberative place to learn. In sisterhood, we found our sanctuary. I learned much alongside my research partners and, as a result, offer wisdom and insight from our truth space as steppingstones to institutional change.

Incorporate Black Oral and Literary Traditions

I found the Blue Diamonds were particularly responsive when I utilized Black oral and literary traditions to support them in recognizing, interrogating, and challenging misrepresentations of the Black girl form. We used storytelling, music, and movement to make literacy an interactive process – which stands in marked contrast to the sedentary literacy instruction occurring in most classrooms (Boutte, 2015; Fisher, 2005; Gay, 2010; Grant, Brown, & Brown, 2015; Kinloch, 2018; Love, 2020). For example, having the girls examine the picture books *Hair Dance!* (Johnson, 2007), *My People* (Hughes & Smith, 2009), and *Dancing in the Wings* (Allen, 2000) as a testament to the commonalities and possibilities which exist within the Black experience.

Furthermore, Black literary texts can serve as mentors for building critical content skills but also for navigating the gauntlet of issues and challenges that come with being Black and a girl in a space which was never designed for them (Boutte, 2015; Johnson et al., 2018; King & Swartz, 2015). In addition, truth spaces allow students to bring their digital lives and literacy footprints into the classroom. Finally, the Blue Diamond truth space can reaffirm the power of owning and loving our Blackness by affording Black girls opportunities to speak their truths in a creative manner, be it art, poetry, photography, or music; emphasizing and affirming the notion there is no one way to tell a story and that art and writing can be used to communicate, advocate, as well as heal. Opportunities for thoughtful analysis of texts through multiple critical readings can allow students to create a re-envisioning of the Black girl form while promoting sisterhood, community, agency, and creativity. As was found, embodying truth spaces, there is potential for Black Girls to be transformed from passive, compliant students to active, responsible, knowledgeable activists whose lives serve as testimony to the resilience of the Black spirit.

Engage in Critical Study That Names and Confronts Injustice

This task cannot be taken lightly nor can it be assumed that being a Black woman is the sole qualifier to create a humanizing, critical, and creative group. To create a truth space involves an introspective criticality where internalized racisms are openly named and confronted (Kohli, 2013; Kohli, Johnson, & Perez, 2006). This space for resistance is imperative as it nurtures the idea of multifaceted and varied perceptions of beauty. Townsend, Thomas, and Jackson-Lowman (2013) asserted:

> As one African American proverb suggests: "Beauty is as beauty does" …. a single monolithic standard of beauty is untenable; it makes no sense. Nature, with its phenomenal diversity, provides a model of the range and variety that beauty may assume. Thus, a lily is no more beautiful than a rose; an oak tree no more beautiful than a palm tree; and an opal no more beautiful than a pearl. Each is beautiful in its own right and each has unique value and plays a special role in nature.
>
> (p. 169)

This message of love, openness, and acceptance is needed to counteract the hegemonic beauty standard.

Build a Trusting Environment

Whether working with adolescents, preservice teachers, or colleagues, truth spaces must be constructed where group members are willing to be openly transparent and share their stories of healing and experiences of trauma. Furthermore, educators must model and exemplify activism by denouncing racist, sexist, sizist acts occurring within the school walls. This action is a cornerstone of building trust as one cannot trust an individual who ignores or overlooks suffering.

When I began to craft this Implications chapter, I contacted the Blue Diamond girls to seek their assistance. I asked them, "What would you like teachers to do in order to better Support Black adolescent girls?" Their responses came quickly, and all revolved around the same theme: "Speaking the truth." For the girls, this meant teachers acknowledging their current realities which include speaking out against unjust and dehumanizing acts. Throughout our time together, the girls repeatedly asked teachers for assistance and were repeatedly denied. Oftentimes, this denial came with the advice that they should pick their battles carefully.

This advice, however, teaches impressionable minds that there are some acts of injustice, which are deemed tolerable. This myth only reifies an oppressive construct. Instead of ignoring or underplaying these experiences, educator activists must acknowledge and disavow these acts.

If educators are truly committed to educational equity, they must ensure they receive continuous personal and professional development focused on courageous conversations about race, patriarchy, power, and privilege, implementing a culturally relevant curriculum, and analyzing programs and policies to ensure they are inclusionary and celebrate Blackness (Boutte, 2015; Gay, 2010; Grant et al., 2015; King, 2005). It is important to note the word "continuous" as often these professional developments are conducted in a "one and done" manner. Yet, the commitment creating truth spaces for educational equity and is a long-term fight and cannot be achieved with such a mindset. Educators must commit to ongoing and continuous personal and professional development.

Commit to Being an Educator-Activist

As I reflect on our truth space, I realized I was more than a mere educator. By providing the opportunity for the Blue Diamond girls to critically analyze the world and the word (Freire & Macedo, 1987), share their stories of racist and sexist experiences, and provide advice to future sisters, I was a truth warrior and educator activist. This role moves beyond teaching content to teaching skills and strategies necessary to critique and challenge hegemonic principles. Although Black women educators are leading the charges, white women educators, the predominant presence in the teaching workforce, are not absolved from the work. Nor should they believe the myth of fragility to dissuade them from taking on this task. As Bettina Love (2020) states, it takes courage and fortitude to build, benefit, and capitalize on oppression. Repurpose the courage and fortitude in the service of others and become a truth warrior. The members of the Blue Diamond truth space clearly display how ignoring unjust acts and eliminating crucial conversations about race, gender, size, privilege, and power created pain, mistrust, and trauma. As such, truth warriors and educator activists must also pledge to, "first do no harm" (Diekelmann, 2002) by vowing to take on the mantle of humanizing and critical social justice work (Freire, 2000) as truth warriors. In this role, we cannot randomly select the social issues which please us, but must wholeheartedly commit to recognizing, seeing, and loving all children.

To be a truth warrior, teachers and teacher educators must first decenter whiteness for themselves and for their students. Within our truth space, the Blue Diamond girls and I deconstructed hegemonic beauty ideals. Whenever texts were read, we did not simply consume them; we completed a thorough examination of content and asked the question: Whose voice was silenced, maligned, or marginalized? For example, when analyzing a Sports *Illustrated Cover* which featured Barbie, Amir asked the "Why does Barbie the only ideal for perfection? My doll Kenya was just as beautiful. Where her cover at?" Such discussions vocalized the need for affirming cultural texts. This statement reaffirms the need for positive and inspiring culturally relevant texts.

In addition, a modification of these questions was used as a lens to analyze their experiences guide by asking, how did it feel to be ignored? How did it feel to be silenced? Why must we stop these actions? Through their stories, we courageously faced what many deemed taboos and engaged in critical conversations about race, gender, size, and power (Cox, 2020; Kinloch, 2018).

I know that as readers review the implications chapters they might inquire: How do I engage in a truth space? What should I begin to read? Such a reader would look to the implications to be a how-to document detailing step-by-step instructions. Yet, such a practice goes against a truth space's intent because being intentional and purposeful critically is an individualized journey which begins with the introspection of naming privileges, biases, and long-standing power structures (Bell, 1992; Collins, 2000; hooks, 1995; Lorde, 1984; Moore, 2018). This is the criticality which undergirds my theoretical frameworks: Critical Race Theory and Black Feminist Thought. Both frameworks believe that critical thinking, critical learning, and critical transformation cannot be plotted on a map. Instead, they must be based in hearing, understanding, learning, and knowing the stories and wisdom of people of Color (Bell, 1992; Collins, 2000; Delgado, Stefancic, & Harris, 2017; Lorde, 1984). It is this experiential knowledge which serves as a powerful counterstory to dominant and oppressive narratives which imbue classrooms and curriculums (Apugo, Mawhinney, Mbilishaka, & Dixson, 2020; Boutte, 2015; Johnson et al., 2018; King & Swartz, 2015; Kinloch, 2005, 2018; Love, 2020; Muhammad, 2020). As mentioned earlier, this book serves as a counternarrative to traditional academic research and I grounded it in the works and knowledge of Critical Theorists who have come before. I would ask the readers to look to their wisdom as I did.

Reflect Regularly

I also want to leave the reader with guiding questions to promote their introspection. For this, I will ask additional questions to those offered in Chapter 3. I ask you once again to pause and reflect upon your personal and professional choices. These questions are to push you beyond the superficiality of performative allyship. I ask you to stare deeply into the depths of your soul and contemplate the following:

- Do I demonstrate teaching with a love ethic when I refuse to discuss racism and oppression in my classroom?
- Do I demonstrate teaching with a love ethic when I refuse to discuss racism and oppression with families and friends?

- Do I demonstrate teaching with a love ethic when I fail to acknowledge my biases and privileges?
- Do I demonstrate teaching with a love ethic when I turn away from an issue because it may demand that I forfeit my securities?
- Do I demonstrate teaching with a love ethic when I display histories and literatures that minimize the atrocities and contradictory behavior of historical/contemporary figures?
- Do I demonstrate a love ethic when I fail to learn more about my students' many situated identities?
- Do I demonstrate a love ethic when I fail to research and learn more about racism, sexism, and sizism?
- Do I demonstrate a love ethic when I ask Black students or colleagues to provide a roadmap to a critical awakening?
- Do I demonstrate a love ethic when I fail to leave my community in order to learn more about students, families, and their communities?
- Do I demonstrate a love ethic when I refuse to alter curricula, pedagogies, and discussions to celebrate Black writers, but in particular, Black women writers as a dominant element in the normalized curriculum (not just for a unit of study)?
- Do I demonstrate a love ethic when I fail to leverage my status to garner another's freedom?
- Do I demonstrate a love ethic when I avoid conversations on racism, sexism, or sizism because it makes me uncomfortable?
- Do I demonstrate a love ethic when I refuse to bear witness to the lived experiences of Black girls/women?
- Do I demonstrate a love ethic when I fail to see beyond being a "good" person instead of asking: How can a good person still contribute to and benefit from systemic racism?

These questions are not to use once and proclaim yourself healed or woke or a social justice teacher. These are not labels to be picked up and used haphazardly. Committing to this work means owning you will forever be a work in progress. Committing to this work means revisiting these questions time and time again. Committing to this work means offering your privileges as sacrifice to be in the service of others. Committing to this work means getting comfortable with being uncomfortable because. For most educators who are white, we are building a world in which you are not the center. A world which has not existed before. A world in which Black lives are loved, lauded, and protected.

Finally, I came to this inquiry because I was hurting, and I observed my students in pain. I came to theory because I was angry at the realities which stood before me. Black adolescent girls hold a precarious position in America: their stories silenced, their bodies objectified, brutalized, and murdered (Apugo et al., 2020; Chang, 2016; Crenshaw et al., 2015; Evans-Winters, 2019; Morris, 2016;

Muhammad & Haddix, 2016). Building on the works of Lorde (1984) and hooks (1995) who postulate anger and rage as a legitimate response to racism, sexism, and other forms of oppression, such as sizism, I ask: Where is the anger? Where is the rage?

Concluding Thoughts

> No black woman writer in this culture can write "too much". Indeed, no woman writer can write "too much"…. No woman has ever written enough.
> ~bell hooks

I began this inquiry because I was wounded and saw that students around me were wounded as well. I knew that schooling could be a better place in support of young Black women who were negotiating intersections of race, gender, and size. So, I sought insight from the experts: Black adolescent girls. I not only found wisdom; I, like they, found sanctuary. We were all hesitant in sharing our stories, but collectively we realized, we were not alone; and speaking our stories, gave them power. The Blue Diamond truth space was empirically important in many ways, not the least of which was its therapeutic nature.

The creation of this critical, humanizing, and creative truth space revealed insights into ways five Black adolescent girls negotiated the intricacies of their lives comprised on intersections of race, gender, and size. Through their honest revelations and poignant counternarratives, I learned more about the educational contested spaces and environments needed to promote educational equity and excellence. Our truth space was firmly cemented in a resolve to listen and learn from the stories that were shared grounded in a commitment to Alice Walker's warning that "if you deny people a voice …. their own voice, there is no way you will ever know who they were" (Powers & Gates, 2013, p. 445). Since to truly know our students we must listen to their voices, more research that engages student voices is critical. As I think about the experiences of Black girls throughout this nation, I realized this therapy, this sanctuary is vital for resilience, rejuvenation, and revitalizing education.

Writing this book was a rite of passage for me. I opened my soul and my stories to the Blue Diamond girls, my editors, and other readers. Throughout the process, I repeatedly asked myself: Am I revealing too much? Am I writing too much truth? When these doubts arose, I took comfort in bell hooks' words, "No black woman writer in this culture can write too much. Indeed, no woman writer can write too much … No woman has ever written enough" (Powers & Gates, 2013, p. 488). These words, like the words of my other wisdom warriors, grounded me because I realized, it is our stories that will lead to understanding; it is our stories that will lead to healing; it is our stories that will restore and rebuild; it is our stories that will lead to transformation. Our stories are and will forever remain, love, hope, and possibility.

References

Allen, D. (2000). *Dancing in the wings*. Dial Books for Young Readers.
Angelou, M. (1970). *I know why the caged bird sings*. Random House.
Apugo, D., Mawhinney, L., Mbilishaka, A., & Dixson, A. (2020). *Strong black girls: Reclaiming schools in their own image*. Teachers College Press.
Battle, N. T. (2021). *Black girlhood, punishment, and resistance (intersectional criminology)* (1st ed.). Routledge.
Beale, F. (1971). *Double jeopardy: To be Black and female*. Radical Education Project.
Bell, D. (1992). *Faces at the bottom of the well: The permanence of racism*. Basic Books.
Boutte, G. (2015). *Educating African American students: And how are the children?* Routledge.
Chang, C. (2016). How Black girls are locked out of America's schools. *The New Republic*. Retrieved from https://newrepublic.com/article/136390/birth-conservative-media-know
Collins, P. H. (2000). *Black feminist thought: Knowledge, consciousness, and the politics of empowerment*. Routledge.
Cox, J. (2020). *Fat girls in black bodies: Creating communities of our own*. North Atlantic
Crenshaw, K., Ocen, P., & Nanda, K. (2015). *Black girls matter: Pushed out, overpoliced, and underprotected* (pp. 1–29, Rep.). African-American Policy Reform.
Delgado, R., Stefancic, J., & Harris, A. P. (2017). *Critical race theory: An introduction*. New York University Press.
Diekelmann, N. L. (2002). *First, do no harm: Power, oppression, and violence in healthcare*. University of Wisconsin Press.
DuBois, W. E. (1903). The souls of black folk; essays and sketches. *Chicago, A. G. McClurg*, 1903. Johnson Reprint.
Evans-Winters, V. E. (2011). *Teaching Black girls: Resiliency in urban classrooms*. P. Lang.
Evans-Winters, V. E. (2019). *Black feminism in qualitative inquiry: A mosaic for writing our daughters body*. Routledge.
Fisher, M. T. (2005). From the coffee house to the school house: The promise and potential of spoken word poetry in school contexts. *English Education, 37*, 115–131.
Freire, P. (2000). *Pedagogy of the oppressed*. Continuum.
Freire, P., & Macedo, D. P. (1987). *Literacy: Reading the word and the world*. Bergin & Garvey.
Gay, G. (2010). *Culturally responsive teaching: Theory, research, and practice*. Teachers College Press.
Grant, C. A., Brown, K. D., & Brown, A. L. (2015). *Black intellectual thought in education: The missing traditions of Anna Julia Cooper, Carter G. Woodson, and Alain Leroy Locke*. Routledge.
Hooks, B. (1990). *Yearning: Race, gender, and cultural politics*. South End Press.
Hooks, B. (1992). *Black looks: Race and representation*. South End Press.
Hooks, B. (1995). *Killing rage: Ending racism*. Holt, Henry & Company, Inc.
Hooks, B. (2012). *All about love: New visions*. William Morrow.
Hughes, L., & Smith, C. R. (2009). *My people*. Atheneum Books for Young Readers Books.
Johnson, D. (2007). *Hair dance!* Henry Holt.
Johnson, L. L., Boutte, G., Greene, G., & Smith, D. E. (2018). *African diaspora literacy: The heart of transformation in K-12 schools and teacher education*. Books, an imprint of The Rowman & Littlefield Publishing Group.
Johnson, L. L., Bryan, N., & Boutte, G. (2018). Show us the love: Revolutionary teaching in (un) critical times. *The Urban Review, 51*(1), 46–64. doi:10.1007/s11256-018-0488-3.
King, J. E. (2005). *Black education: A transformative research and action agenda for the new century*. L. Erlbaum.

King, J. E., & Swartz, E. (2015). *The Afrocentric praxis of teaching for freedom: Connecting culture to learning*. Routledge.

Kinloch, V. (2005). Poetry, literacy, and creativity: Fostering effective learning strategies in an urban classroom. *English Education, 37*, 96–114.

Kinloch, V. (2018). Commitment and danger, Black life and Black love: Toward radical possibilities. *Taboo: The Journal of Culture and Education, 17*(1), 69–78. doi:10.31390/taboo.17.1.08

Kohli, R. (2013). Unpacking internalized racism: Teachers of color striving for racially just classrooms. *Race Ethnicity and Education, 17*(3), 367–387.

Kohli, R., Johnson, R. N., & Perez, L. H. (2006). Naming racism: A conceptual look at internalized racism in U.S. schools. *Chicano-Latino Law Review, 25*, 183–206.

Logan, R. (2014, August). This grandma thinks the school district went too far. *Newsone*. http://newsone.com/3042380/kenji-roberts-henry-county-school-district/

Lorde, A. (1984). *Sister outsider: Essays and speeches*. Crossing Press.

Love, B. (2020). *We want to do more than survive: Abolitionist teaching and the pursuit of educational freedom*. Beacon Press.

Lyiscott, J. (2020). Fugitive literacies as inscriptions of freedom. *English Education, 52*(3), 256–263.

Moore, D. L. (2018). Black radical love: A practice. *Public Integrity, 20*(4), 325–328. doi:10.1080/10999922.2018.1439564

Morris, M. W. (2016). *Pushout: The criminalization of Black girls in schools*. The New Press.

Morris, M. W. (2019). *Sing a rhythm, dance a blues: Education for the liberation of Black and Brown girls*. The New Press.

Morrison, T. (1994). *The bluest eye*. Plume Book.

Muhammad, G. (2020). *Cultivating genius: An equity framework for culturally and historically responsive literacy*. Scholastic.

Muhammad, G., & Haddix, M. (2016). Centering Black girls' literacies: A review of literature on the multiple ways of knowing of Black girls. *English Education, 48*(4), 229–336.

Ohito, E. (2020). "The creative aspect woke me up": Awakening to multimodal essay composition as a fugitive literacy practice. *English Education, 52*(3), 186–222.

Powers, R., & Gates, H. L. (2013). *Bartlett's familiar black quotations*. Little Brown and Company.

Schott Foundation for Public Education. (2016). *The urgency of now: The Schott 50 state report on public education and Black males*. (Rep.). Cambridge University Press.

Soichet, C., Fantz, A., & Yan, H. (2015, June 10). Texas officer's attorney: He let his emotions get the better of him. *CNN*. http://www.cnn.com/2015/06/10/us/mckinney-texas-pool-party-video/

Townsend, T. G., Thomas, A. J., & Jackson-Lowman, H. (2013). Jezebel's legacy: The development of African American heterosexual girls' emerging sexuality in the context of oppressive images and the armoring influence of mother-daughter relationships. In H. Jackson-Lowman (Ed.), *Afrikan American women: Living at the crossroads of race, gender, class, and culture*. Cognella Academic Publishing.

Webb, K. (2013, March). 8-year-old arrested, handcuffed for tantrum at school. *Atlanta Black Star*. http://atlantablackstar.com/2013/03/08/eight-year-old-special-needs-student-arrested-in-illinois/

APPENDIX
METHODOLOGICAL DETAILS

odo nyera

The research design for this study utilized critical race narrative, ethnopoetics, and auto-ethnography methodologies to explore and document how an eighth-grade literature truth space responded to depictions of obesity in adolescent literature and media for the purpose of providing insights on how adolescent literature discussion groups can be utilized to analyze societal constructs regarding the confluence of messages about size, gender, and race.

Rationale: Methodological Stance

To develop a qualitative methodological stance, I drew upon my knowledge of auto-ethnography, critical race counternarrative, and arts-based research – specifically ethnopoetics. explained below.

Autoethnography

Autoethnography is a qualitative method which blends the characteristics of autobiography and ethnography (Boylorn & Orbe, 2017). Autoethnography builds upon the idea of transformation because it alters time allowing past events to be viewed and analyzed from several different perspectives including event member and researcher in the present; engages vulnerability helping to clarify purpose; embodies creativity and innovation as it allows unique experiences – in this case by experiences with racism, gender bias, and sizism to be illuminated, reviewed and redefined (Boylorn & Orbe, 2017). Utilizing autoethnography permits the production of evocative personal and interpersonal memories by having the researcher discern patterns of her or his own experience (Beach, Bagley, & Silva, 2018; hooks, 1994). Incorporating such a methodology not only allowed me to examine and share my personal stories related to race, body image, and gender, it also allowed me to serve as a witness (Denzin, 2016; Ellis & Bochner, 2006; Weaver-Hightower, 2018) for the brutal and often subtle cruelties of the obesity experience and a co-narrator with the students as we examined texts to hopefully validate others and inspire change.

Critical Race Counternarratives

Delgado, Stefancic, and Harris (2017) define counternarratives in the service of Critical Race Theory (CRT) as the telling the stories of marginalized individuals, which serve as sites and stories of resistance. Counternarratives recognize the rich history of storytelling in African and African American heritage and build upon the myriad of unheard and untold stories and experiences for people of Color. Since stories are told in a variety of manners, counternarratives exist in a variety of styles including personal stories, narratives, and composite stories (Beach et al., 2018; Bell, 1992; Cook, 2013). Solórzano and Yosso (2002) declared, "Counter-stories can shatter complacency, challenge the dominant discourse on race and further the struggle for racial reform" (p. 32). In essence, racist ideology creates and strengthens the "master narrative" which perpetuates privileges for white girls/women and the idea of thin and beautiful being synonymous. This oppressive ideology silences voices of Color and erodes Black beauty values and beliefs. The power of counternarratives lies in their ability to speak back and critique the majoritarian narrative and proudly declares that white privilege cannot and does not allow the right to tell a story which is not yours (Bell, 1992; Delgado et al., 2017). By emphasizing experiential knowledge from people of Color, counternarratives allow for the witnessing of truths long silenced as it critiques social, political, and cultural constructs.

Critical race counternarrative was foundational to my methodology because it provided a way for me to capture the voices of my research partners. Delgado (2002) affirmed "an emphasis on experiential knowledge also allows researchers to embrace the use of counterstories, narratives, testimonios, and oral histories to illuminate the unique experiences of students of Color" (p. 109). In traditional educational approaches, experiential knowledge of oppressed and marginalized people is regularly viewed and dismissed as a deficit (Boutte, 2015; Ellison & Solomon, 2019; Johnson, Boutte, Greene, & Smith, 2018). CRT, however, proudly proclaims it as a strength that must be heard, validated, and acted upon. Embracing such a methodology allows researchers to strive to create contexts in which research partners may speak their truths – share and utilize experiential knowledge – in a manner which is both comfortable and heart-felt, reaffirming their positions as creators and holders of knowledge. This opportunity was at the foundation of the literature discussion sessions I designed for and with this study's research partners (the students), creating rich contexts for the collection and analysis of data and our consideration of action for the future.

Ethnopoetics

Barone and Eisner (2011) affirmed arts-based research as a methodology that allows researchers to "revisit the world from a different direction, seeing it with fresh eyes and thereby calling into question a singular orthodox point of view" (p. 16). For this study, I draw on the arts by using ethnopoetics as a methodological tool. Given (2008) described ethnopoetics as a verbal art form which exists in all languages and cultures and utilizes such techniques as prayers, chants, and praises. Ethnopoetics allowed me to analyze and represent data in ways which have the potential to cast a new light on issues of body image, race, and gender. As a resistance platform, ethnopoems assert poetry as a truth-bearing and deconstructive tool which challenges the idea of "normality" because for there to be a normal an "other" must exist (Collins, 2015). In particular, because normalized, singular Western views of body image have long served as social markers of acceptance, a moral barometer, and a tool of marginalization and disenfranchisement (Murray, 2005), ethnopoetics provided an opportunity for me to revisit the world from a different direction as I called into question orthodoxies that view the obese form as a transgression of "acceptable" boundaries, as not normal (Patterson-Faye, 2016). In a discourse and construct where overweight or obese bodies are read as a moral and physical violation and where race and gender are melded into a singular social identity, experiential knowledge articulated through ethnopoetics allows for a reimagining of the body. Ethnopoetics is a perfect tool to create such moments as different poetic forms create new meaning and new understandings (Barone & Eisner, 2011; Leavy, 2020).

Context and Participants

This study was conducted at a middle school in the Southeastern United States, where data were collected after school hours during a truth space that I facilitated with five eighth-grade girls. Those contexts are detailed in Chapter 4.

Selection of Participants

I utilized criterion sampling for research partner/group member selection. Patton (2001) defined criterion sampling as the researcher's attempt to, "review and study all cases that meet some predetermined criterion of importance" (p. 238). The five research partners were selected based on several criteria including (a) race, (b) gender, (c) grade-level attainment, and (d) participation in the middle school afterschool program.

Obtaining Partner Consent

Letters were sent home to the research partners' families requesting permission to allow their children to participate in an afterschool truth circle which would focus on how adolescents respond to body image, gender, and race in adolescent texts. The letter identified this study's goals and provided a brief description of its parameters as well as explaining the benefits of participating which included the academic skills students would learn while participating. The letter also explained how participating in this project had the potential to provide a greater understanding of the ways negotiating race, gender, and size could impact educational practices. The letter informed parents all interviews and other materials would remain confidential and explained that under no circumstances would data be shared with anyone without their explicit permission, nor would research partners experience any discomfort as a result of participation in this study. The letter described how the results of this research project may be presented at academic conferences, professional meetings, or in publications; however, pseudonyms would be used for the students and the school. Finally, the letter stated that their children's involvement was entirely voluntary, and they had the right to discontinue participation at any time. The signed parental permission forms are kept in a locked file cabinet in my office. I have the only key to this cabinet.

Obtaining Human Subjects Approval (IRB)

I submitted my Human Subjects Approval plan to the Institutional Review Board (IRB) at the same time I submitted this proposal to my dissertation committee. The plan contained a description of the study, questions, research partners, and data collection methods. The plan also included sample student consent forms and described methods of ensuring safety and privacy. The proposal was approved on April 15, 2015.

Data Collection Methods

A variety of data collection methods were utilized in this study. Data were collected in the forms of semi-structured interviews, truth circle discussions; students' counternarratives, students' journaling, researcher's field journal, and my own poetry. The chart below illustrates the research questions for the study as they were aligned with data sources and my methods of analysis. Detailed descriptions of each method are provided in Chapter 4.

Appendix

Research Questions, Data Sources, and Analysis

Research Questions	Data Sources	Method of Analysis
1. How do a group of five eighth-grade African American girls at a middle school in the southeastern United States (Houston Middle School, pseudonym) respond to portrayals of size, race, and gender in adolescent texts and media?	• Literature Study Artifacts • Research Partner Journals • Field Journal/Research Journal • Semi-structured individual interviews • Audio-Recordings of Sessions	• Protocol coding, In Vivo coding of journals, field notes, transcriptions, and observations to identify how the members' perceptions and beliefs about race, gender, and body size changed throughout the study • Descriptive coding, Protocol coding, Emotional coding and In Vivo coding of truth circle artifacts, transcriptions, and journals
2. How do these portrayals impact the girls and their identities and literacy practices?	• Literature Study Artifacts • Research Partner Journals • Field Journal/Research Journal • semi-structured individual interviews • Audio-Recordings of Sessions	• Protocol coding, In Vivo coding of journals, field notes, transcriptions, and observations to identify how obesity/body image portrayals impact their identities and literacy practices • Descriptive coding, Protocol coding, Emotional coding, and In Vivo coding of truth circle artifacts, transcriptions, and journals
3. What happens when they are given the opportunity to create counternarratives about gender, race, and obesity?	• Counternarratives • Research Partner Journals • Field Journal/Research Journal • Semi-structured individual interviews • Audio-Recordings of Sessions	• Protocol coding, In Vivo coding of journals, field notes, transcriptions, and observations to identify how girls experienced the process of creating counternarratives • Descriptive coding, Protocol coding, Emotional coding, and In Vivo coding of counternarratives, transcriptions, and journals

Data Organization

Data were collected electronically and downloaded into folders on my computer. The journals were spiral notebooks. Each individual journal was scanned and placed into a folder titled with each of the girls' names. Each folder was password-protected to ensure confidentiality. I also backed up data on an external drive, both of which required passwords to access study files. Hard copies of journals and artifacts were organized chronologically into folders which was an important way to back up and store data. All data were kept in a secure location – my locked office at home and/or at work – to ensure confidentiality.

See Chapter 4 for a description of Data Coding and Analysis, Triangulation, and Positionality.

Timeline

This study from conception to defense covered a six-week period. The timeline below displays the timeframe for the initiation of the study through the dissertation defense.

Research Timeline

March 2015	*Met with Afterschool Coordinator*
	Met with Afterschool Teachers
	Member Selection
April 2015	*Mail Research Partner Parent Approval Letters*
	Truth circles Meetings were initiated.
	Week One
	• April 21st from 4:30 to 6:00
	• April 22nd from 4:30 to 6:00
	• April 23rd from 4:30 to 6:00
	Week Two
	• April 28th from 4:30 to 6:00
	• Member Checking/Share with Committee
	• April 29th from 4:30 to 6:00
	• April 30th from 4:30 to 6:00

May 2015	*Truth circles continued:*
	Week Three:
	May 5th
	• May 6th from 4:30 to 6:00
	• Initial member checking/
	• May 7th from 4:30 to 6:00
	Week Four:
	• May 12th from 4:30 to 6:00
	• May 13th from 4:30 to 6:00
	• May 14th from 4:30 to 6:00
	• Member Checking
	Week Five:
	• May 19th from 4:30 to 6:00
	• May 20th from 4:30 to 6:00
	• May 21st from 4:30 to 6:00
	• Member Checking
	Week Six:
	• May 28th from 4:30 to 6:00
June–December 2015	Data Analysis
	Final Member Checking
January–October 2016	Writing the Dissertation
October 27, 2016	Dissertation Defense

References

Barone, T., & Eisner, E. W. (2011). *Arts based research.* SAGE.

Beach, D., Bagley, C., & Silva, S. M. (2018). *The Wiley handbook of ethnography of education.* John Wiley & Sons.

Bell, D. (1992). *Faces at the bottom of the well: The permanence of racism.* Basic Books.

Boutte, G. (2015). *Educating African American students: And how are the children?* Routledge.

Boylorn, R. M., & Orbe, M. P. (2017). *Critical autoethnography: Intersecting cultural identities in everyday life.* Routledge.

Collins, P. H. (2015). *Black feminist thought: Knowledge, consciousness, and the politics of empowerment*. Routledge, Taylor & Francis Group.

Cook, D. A. (2013). Blurring the boundaries: The mechanics of creating composite characters. In M. Lynn & A. Dixson (Eds.), *Handbook of critical race theory in education: CRT and innovations in educational research methodologies* (pp. 181–194). Routledge.

Delgado, R. (2002). Derrick Bell's toolkit—fit to dismantle that famous house. *University Law Review, 75*(2), 283–307.

Delgado, R., Stefancic, J., & Harris, A. P. (2017). *Critical race theory: An introduction*. New York University Press.

Denzin, N. K. (2016). *Qualitative inquiry through a critical lens*. Routledge.

Ellis, C. S., & Bochner, A. P. (2006). Analyzing analytic autoethnography. *Journal of Contemporary Ethnography, 35*(4), 429–449. doi:10.1177/0891241606286979

Ellison, T., & Solomon, M. (2019). Counter-storytelling vs. deficit thinking counter-storytelling vs. deficit thinking around African American children and families, digital literacies, race, and the digital divide. *Research in the Teaching of English, 53*(3), 223–244.

Given, L. M. (2008). *The Sage encyclopedia of qualitative research methods*. Sage.

hooks, b. (1994). *Teaching to Transgress*. Routledge.

Johnson, L. L., Boutte, G., Greene, G., & Smith, D. E. (2018). *African diaspora literacy: The heart of transformation in K-12 schools and teacher education*. Lexington Books, an imprint of The Rowman & Littlefield Publishing Group.

Leavy, P. (2020). *Method meets art: Arts-based research practice*. The Guilford Press.

Murray, S. (2005). (Un/Be) coming out? Rethinking fat politics. *Social Semiotics, 15*(2), 153–163. doi:10.1080/10350330500154667

Patterson-Faye, C. J. (2016). 'I like the way you move': Theorizing fat, black and sexy. *Sexualities, 19*(8), 926–944. doi:10.1177/1363460716640731

Patton, M. Q. (2001). *Qualitative research and evaluation methods*. Sage Publications.

Solórzano, D. G., & Yosso, T. J. (2002). Critical race methodology: Counter-storytelling as an analytical framework for education research. *Qualitative Inquiry, 8*(1), 23–44. doi:10.1177/107780040200800103

Weaver-Hightower, M. B. (2018). Analyzing self and other in autoethnography. *How Qualitative Data Analysis Happens*, 3–17. doi:10.4324/9781315171647-1

INDEX

Pages in *italics* refer figures, **bold** refer tables and pages followed by n refer notes

Acevedo, E. 64
Adichie, C. 40
African American girls 14
African American Policy Forum (AAPF) 31
African dancers 3
African notion of Ubuntu 13
Agape love 13
Aguilera, C. 139
Alice, M. 135
All About Love 44
Alvarez, A. 104n5, 104n7
American Library Association 14
Anderson, T. 32
Angelou, M. 109, 150
Arbery, A. 31
Atta, D. 64

Baker-Bell, A. 11
Baldwin, J. 44, 113
Barak, G. 18
Barone, T. 161
Baszile, D. T. 42
Beale, F. 38
Bell, D. 31–32, 36, 104n16
Bergner, G. 124
Berry, D. C. 126
The Biggest Loser 21
Bishop, R. S. 125
Black adolescent girls 23, 40, 57, 59, 148, 152, 155–156

Black and Brown bodies 149
Black Feminist Studies 38–40; black frame 39; *Black Looks: Race and Representation* 39; feminist theorist 39; participation 40; principle of intersectionality 39; suffering and marginalization of women 39; white frame 39
Black Feminist Thought 13, 35, *35*
The Black Flamingo 64
Black Girl Literacies Collective (BGLC) 10–11
Black Intellectual Thought 107
Black literary heritage 42, *141*, 147
Black Looks: Race and Representation 39
Bland, S. 32
Blue Diamonds 16–17; analysis 60–62; descriptive codes **61**; healing lessons 52; interviews 58–60; journal and notes 60; positionality 62–63; truth circle members *see* Blue Diamond Truth Circle; verse novel 64–65
Blue Diamond Truth Circle 54–58; creating counternarratives 56; journaling supplies 56–57, *57*; research supplies 57–58, *58*; structured format 56; text selection **55**; truth spaces artifacts 54, 56
The Bluest Eye 147
Boutte, G. 48–49, 62, 64, 66, 111, 122, 130, 133, 137, 144

168 Index

Boyd, R. 32
Brown Girl Dreaming 64
Bryant, M. 32
Bumpurs, E. 32
Butler, T. 11

Cahnman, W. 18
Carey, M. 32
characterization chart **112**
Chea, M. 11
Christian, A. 32
The Chronicle of the Sacrificed Black Child 32
Cite Black Women Movement 33
Clarke, M. 124
Collins, A. M. 30
Collins, P. H. 38–39, 127, 133, 136
The Color Complex 123–126
colorism: A Black Out Poem 81; *The Color Complex* 123–126; Dark Girls: A Poem in Two Voices 82–83, 126; A Definition Poem 80–81, 123; Heart's Desire: Colorism in Action 83–84, 126–128; Researcher's Note 84–86, 128; skin tone scale *124*
comprehension and discernment 10
contextualizing implications *147*
counternarratives: Body Love: An Autobiography in Five Short Chapters 101–103, 140; A Definition Poem 98–99, 137–138; Fat: A Counternarrative in Visual Form 100, 138; Greater is Coming: Praise in Lyrics and Movement 101, 139–140; methodological approach 137; Naming Myself: A Body Visual Poem 137; picture books 137; Power Playlist 138, **139**
Covid-19 pandemic: America's response to 29–30; complications 28
Cox, J. 19, 104n3
Crenshaw, K. 36, 39, 104n9–n10, 129
Critical Race Theory (CRT) 13, 35–38, 65
Crow, J. 52
Cullen, C. 104n13
Culp, J. 38
Cussesaux, M. 32

Daniels, D. 32
dark black leather 2
Davis, A. 38
Davis, S. 32
Dawkins, R. 118
deafening screams 3

A Definition Poem: colorism 80–81, 123; counternarratives 98–99, 137–138; fat 72, 114, 116–118; intersectionality 86, 129
Delgado, R. 36, 38, 104n17–n19, 123, 132, 160
descriptive codes **61**
Dillard, C. 13
Dotson, K. 46
Dove, R. 63
dual lenses 40
Duke, B. 126

Ebony and *Jet Magazines* 2
Edwards, S. 32
Eisner, E. W. 161
English/language arts 6, 15
enslavement 33, 135
Eurocentric and white Supremacist notion 13
Their Eyes Were Watching God 43
Evans-Winters, V. 13, 24, 30, 32, 46–47, 111, 145, 150, 155, 157

fake love, white supremacist society 30–34; America's beliefs 31; America's fake love 33; *Beloved* 30; *The Chronicle of the Sacrificed Black Child* 32; Cite Black Women Movement 33; Cold War Objectives 31; CORE academic syllabi 33; enslavement 33; #SayHerName campaign 31–32
fat: *Autobiography in Five Short Chapters* 118; A Confessional 77–79, 121–122; A Counternarrative in Visual Form 100; A Definition Poem 72, 114, 116–118; meme activity *119*; meme analysis 119, **120**; Researcher's Note 79–80, 122; visual image responses **116**; A Visual Poem 73–77; word association responses **115**
finding sanctuary in truth spaces 23
The Fire Next Time 44
Floyd, G. 31
Fonville, J. 32
Francis, S. 32
Frank, K. 22
Freire, P. 13, 21
Frey, S. 32

Gaines, K. 32
Gee, J. P. 20
Giovanni, N. 108
Golden, P. 32

Good Housekeeping 2
The Gospel According to Shug 42
Greene, D. T. 11
Griffin, A. A. 11
guiding wisdoms, dual lens 40–41

Haddix, M. 11, 151
Haggerty, L. 32
Hall, M. 32
Hall, R. E. 104n8
Hardison, A. 43
Harris, A. P. 127, 160
Hartley, P. 32
Hibbard, K. 22
Higginbotham, E. R. 32
Hilson, K. 139
Hockaday, M. 32
Hodge, R. Y. 11
Hodges, H. 28
hooks, B. 38–40, 44, 108, 140, 156
horrific event into poem 4–6
Houston Middle School 52–53
Houston school's afterschool program 14–16
Houston's Media Center Conference Room *54*
Houston's media specialist 54
Huber, L. 104n14
Hunter, M. 104n6
Hurston, Z. N. 43, 148–149

"If you are silent about your pain," *147*
implications for teachers as truth warriors 150–151; being an educator-activist 153–154; Black oral and literary traditions 151–152; build trust environment 152–153; names and confronts injustice 152; reflect regularly 154–156
intersectionality: Bearing Witness: Life as a Black Girl 129–131; Blessings upon Blessings: The Body as a Source of Conflict 92–96, 135–136; body satisfaction/dissatisfaction responses **134**; A Definition Poem 86, 129; Enabling the System: A Cry for Help Denied 90, 132–133; fragmenting of identity 128; notion of 129; A Pocket Full of Wishes: Attracting the Opposite Sex 91, 133, 135; Remixed: Countee Cullen's Experience in 2015 89–90, 131–132; Researcher's Note 96–98, 136; A Tale of Two Girls: Life as a Black Girl 86–89; What is body image? 91–92, 135

Jackson-Lowman, H. 121, 152
Jackson, M. 30
Jahraymecofasola love 41–45; *All About Love* 44; Black literary heritage 42; Black radical love 41; depths of soul and contemplate 45; *Their Eyes Were Watching God* 43; *The Fire Next Time* 44; *The Gospel According to Shug* 42; reflections on Truth and Love **43**
James, K. 32
Jefferson, A. 30, 32
Jelks, R. 43
Johnson, D. 32
Johnson, K. 30
Johnson, L. L. 18, 20, 23–25, 29–30, 32, 42, 48–49, 66, 111, 122, 130, 137, 144, 149, 151–152
Johnston, K. 32
Jones, S. 11
Jordan, J. 36

Kellner, D. 33
King, J. E. 41
Kinloch, V. 29, 34, 48, 122, 144, 151, 154, 158
Kirkwood, E. 11
Kynard, C. 11

Ladson-Billings, G. 38
Laughter, J. C. 29
"Learning from the 60s," 107
literacy explorations 13
Livingston, K. 32
Lorde, A. 38, 107, 156
Love, B. 11, 153
loving Black girls 45–46
Lynn, C. 139

Macedo, D. P. 13
Marion, J. 30
mask of stoicism 3
Matsuda, M. 36
McArthur, S. A. 11
McCall, L. 104n12
Mcgee, E. O. 104n5, 104n7
McKay, C. 108
McKenna, N. 32
McMasters, H. 29
McNair, C. D. 30
Menakem, R. 42
Miller, R. 32
Miller, T. 32
Milner, H. R. 29, 104n5, 104n7

Mitchell, M. L. 32
Monahan, M. J. 44
Moore, D. L. 41
Moore, K. 32
Moravcsik, A. 64
Morris, N. 32
Morrison, T. 30, 109, 124, 147
Mueller, A. S. 22
Muhammad, G. E. 11, 151
Muller, C. 22
Murray, S. 19

Nash, J. C. 104n11
Nelson, P. 118
Nevarez, G. 32
Nichter, M. 113
Nicole, B. 139
nuances and complexities of truth 10

obese Black girls/women's form 46
Oliver, J. E. 20, 104n1

pain medication 1
Patton, M. Q. 161
Pearson, J. 22
Perkins, F. A. 32
Perry, T. 11
A Poem in Five Stanzas 70–72
poems and analytic decisions: Blue Diamond girls 110–111; characterization chart **112**; composite poems 108; preface 109–110; racism's destruction 113; researcher's note poem 108; self-reflexivity process 111; text annotation revision strategy *110*; truthful transparency 140–141
poetry writing 9–10
The Poet X 64
Price-Dennis, D. 11
Proctor, S. 32

radical love: Black Feminist Studies 38–40; Black Feminist/Womanist Thought 35, *35*; Critical Race Theory (CRT) 36–38; Eurocentric and white Supremacist notion 13; guiding wisdoms, dual lens 40–41; Jahraymecofasola love 41–45; race and racism 36; soul speak 35; world's destruction of Blackness 44
reflections on Truth and Love **43**
Researcher's Note: Delving into Skin 84–86, 128; examining intersectionalities 96–98, 136; Preface to the Novel 69–70; The Skinny on Fat 79–80, 122

Richardson, E. 11
Robertson, C. 30
Rosser, A. 32
Russell-Cole, K. 104n8

Saldana, J. 62
Sanctuary xiv, 6, 12, 23, 32–33, 40, 46, 49, 136, 140–141, 151
Sawyer, L. T. 11
#SayHerName campaign 31–32
Sealey-Ruiz, Y. 11
Share, J 33
skin tone scale *124*
Smith, C. A. 33
Smith, D. E. 1, 13, 16, 28, 52, 107, 146
Smith, L. T. 65
Smith, Y. 32
snowballing sampling 14
Solórzano, D. G. 104n15, 137, 160
The Spring Valley Incident 148, 150
Spruill, A. 32
Stanley-Jones, A. 32
Stefancic, J. 104n18, 160
Stewart, D. 32
story-telling fashion 4
study matters: engaging adolescents 19–20; grounded convections 19; knowingness 19; normalization of thin, white girl/woman's form 17–18; normalized social construct 18; obesity 20–21; polarizing dynamics 20; presumed knowing 19; social inequities 21–23

taste salvation 1
Taylor, B. 31–32, 43
Taylor, S. 32
Taylor, S. R. 104n2
text annotation revision strategy *110*
Thomas, A. 32
Thomas, A. J. 121, 152
Thomas, E. E. 11
Toliver, S. 11
Townsend, T. G. 121, 152
Turner, A. 22

Vaughn, D. 30
verse novel: Blue Diamonds 64–65; CRT and Black Feminist Theory 65–66; ethnopoetic findings 65; ongoing tensions 64

Walker, A. 42
Wesley, C. 30

Western beauty standards 4
white supremacist society, fake love in 30–34; America's beliefs 31; America's fake love 33; *Beloved* 30; *The Chronicle of the Sacrificed Black Child* 32; Cite Black Women Movement 33; Cold War Objectives 31; CORE academic syllabi 33; enslavement 33; #SayHerName campaign 31–32
Williams, M. 32

Wilson, M. 104n8
Wilson, T. 32
Wolohan, S. 31
Womack, E. 11
Woodson, C. G. 140
Woodson, J. 64
Woodson, K. M. 104n4

Yosso, T. J. 104n15, 137, 160